CHRIST IN THE PSALMS

DAVID BAST

Christ in the Psalms

Published by Words of Hope
700 Ball Ave. N.E.
Grand Rapids, MI 49503-1308

Email: woh@woh.org
World Wide Web: www.woh.org

Italics in biblical quotations represent emphasis added by the author.

Edited by Timothy J. Beals
Cover design by Peter Van Regenmorter
Interior design by Steve Gier

Printed in the United States of America

10 9 8 7 6 5 4 3 2 1

First Edition

CHRIST IN THE PSALMS

Contents

Introduction

> The Psalms are the Manna of the Church. As Manna tasted to every man like that that he liked best, so do the Psalms minister Instruction, and satisfaction, to every man, in every emergency and occasion. David was not only a clear Prophet of Christ himself, but a Prophet of every particular Christian; he foretells what I, what any shall do, and suffer, and say. . . . the whole book of Psalms is . . . an ointment poured out upon all sorts of sores . . . a Balm that searches all wounds.[1]

WHY DO CHRISTIANS READ THE PSALMS? We read them for their beauty and poetry, of course, and for the truths they teach us about God. We read (and sing) the Psalms as an aid to worship. No words for worshiping God, thought Calvin, are better than God's words from his Word, which is why for 200 years Reformed folk sang only psalms in worship.

We especially value the Psalms for their devotional use. As John Donne says in the above-quoted passage, the Psalms minister to everyone "in every emergency and occasion." St. Athanasius, the great 4th-century champion of the orthodox Christian faith, made this same point 1,300 years before Donne. Writing to a friend of his named Marcellinus, Athanasius said that a special virtue of the Psalms was that, whatever our mood or condition, we will find ourselves represented in them, along with the right words to express our need. The Psalter, he wrote,

> is like a picture, in which you see yourself portrayed . . . Elsewhere in the Bible you read . . . the Law . . . you listen to the Prophets . . . you . . . learn the doings of the kings and holy men; but in the Psalter, besides all these things, you learn about *yourself.* You find depicted in it all the movements of your soul, all its changes, its ups and downs, its failures and recoveries. Moreover, whatever your particular need or trouble, from this same book you can select a form of words to fit it, so that you do not merely hear and then pass on, but learn the way to remedy your ill. . . . Whether he has kept the Law or whether he has broken it, it is his own doings that the Psalms describe; everyone is bound to find his very self in them and, be he faithful soul or be he sinner, each reads in them descriptions of himself.[2]

The special glory of the Psalms is not only to show us who and what we are, but to help us pray as we ought, and even to give us the words to say, whatever our need or situation. Most of the Bible speaks *to* us from God; the Psalms speak *for* us to God.

But there is another reason for Christians to pay particular attention to the Psalms—one more thing that makes this book extra special for us. As Donne put it, David was "a clear prophet of Christ." This is the book, of all the Old Testament, that speaks most often and clearly of Jesus the Messiah. Once again St. Athanasius explains.

> When we come to the matters of which the Prophets speak—of the coming of the Savior and how, although He is God, He yet should dwell among us—we find that these occur in almost all [the Psalms] . . . Having thus shown that Christ should come in human form, the Psalter goes on to show that He can suffer in the flesh He has assumed.[3]

In other words, it is not just the prophetic books of the Old Testament that point us toward Christ. The Psalms too are full of testimony to his life and work.

As I reflected on this I found myself thinking of some of the many psalms that are directly applied in the New Testament to Jesus Christ. These are not just psalms that remind us in some way of Jesus (like the 23rd, for example), or that could be interpreted in a messianic sense (like Psalm 72), but psalms that are quoted and then explicitly explained by the New Testament writers with reference to Christ. I thought that studying these passages might prove instructive, and could enrich both our reading of the Psalms and our understanding of the New Testament texts that interpret them. The result is this book.

One note about that interpretation. Even a superficial study makes it obvious that the New Testament writers do not interpret the Psalms "literally" following the grammatical-historical method by which a text is interpreted according to its author's intended meaning. Moreover, the psalm texts are not always quoted verbatim by the New Testament writers who cite them. Sometimes they follow the Greek of the Septuagint rather than the Hebrew text. Sometimes they alter wording slightly on their own, to make a quotation more closely conform to their interpretation.

These practices raise questions for our own hermeneutics and exegesis, and perhaps for our understanding of inspiration as well—questions that are more properly dealt with by biblical scholars. But I would want to say this. The canonical, apostolic writers interpret the Psalms in their spiritual sense, or perhaps I should say, their Spirit-inspired sense. When they see Christ in the Psalms, they are reading these texts according to their ultimate Author's intended meaning. In following their readings, we do the same. "For from him and through him and to him are all things. To him be glory forever. Amen!" (ROMANS 11:36).

Chapter 1

CHRIST THE SON

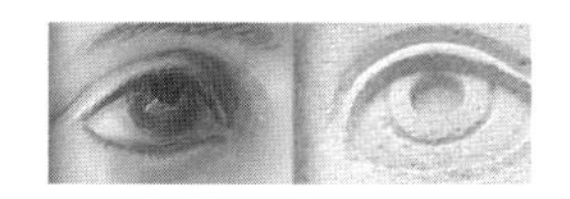

PSALM 2
HEBREWS 1:5

Why do the nations rage
    and the peoples plot in vain?
The kings of the earth set themselves,
    and the rulers take counsel together,
    against the LORD and against his anointed, saying,
"Let us burst their bonds apart
    and cast away their cords from us."

He who sits in the heavens laughs;
    the Lord holds them in derision.
Then he will speak to them in his wrath,
    and terrify them in his fury, saying,
"As for me, I have set my King
    on Zion, my holy hill."

I will tell of the decree: The LORD said to me, "You are my Son;
    today I have begotten you.
Ask of me, and I will make the nations your heritage,
    and the ends of the earth your possession.

You shall break them with a rod of iron
    and dash them in pieces like a potter's vessel."
Now therefore, O kings, be wise;
    be warned, O rulers of the earth.
Serve the LORD with fear,
    and rejoice with trembling.
Kiss the Son,
    lest he be angry, and you perish in the way,
    for his wrath is quickly kindled.
Blessed are all who take refuge in him.

—*Psalm 2*

For to which of the angels did God ever say,
    "You are my Son,
        today I have begotten you"?
Or again,
    "I will be to him a father,
        and he shall be to me a son"?

—*Hebrews 1:5*

"WORDS LIKE 'GOD' AND 'ALLAH' must go the way of 'Apollo' and 'Baal,' or they will unmake our world," states a currently popular book, suggesting that these words and the concepts they represent belong in "the graveyard of bad ideas." A rash of such recently published best sellers have a common theme. They all consist of aggressive attacks on belief in God, combined with a demeaning attitude toward believers. The title of comic Bill Maher's sneering film *Religulous* ("religious" + "ridiculous"—get it?) expresses this attitude clearly.

But atheist manifestos like Sam Harris's *The End of Faith,* from which this chapter's opening quotation was taken, or *The God Delusion* by Richard Dawkins, don't simply argue along standard "I can't believe there's a God" lines. They assert that faith in God of any kind is wrong—not just intellectually wrong, but morally wrong. It's not just that atheists are smart and believers are dumb, according to these writers. (One proposes that people who reject belief in God be known as "brights"; presumably believers, then, are "dims.") It's that believers are bad people. One writer calls the religious instruction of children a form of child abuse. Another of the most virulent of the current anti-God tracts, a book by the British journalist Christopher Hitchens entitled *God Is Not Good,* purports to explain this in its subtitle: *How Religion Poisons Everything.* And Sam Harris implies that anyone who believes in God is essentially a terrorist suicide bomber in the making.

It all brings to mind the ancient question of the psalmist: "Why do the heathen rage . . . against the LORD, and against his anointed?" (PSALM 2:1-2, KJV). Hatred of God and his people is nothing new. Apostles of atheism, those self-appointed bursters of faith's balloon, folks whose chosen mission in life is to set believers free from their "God delusion," have been around for a long, long time. The writer of the second psalm knew well those who rail against God. He asks,

> Why do the nations rage
>   and the peoples plot in vain?
> The kings of the earth set themselves,
>   and the rulers take counsel together,
>   against the LORD and against his anointed, saying,
> "Let us burst their bonds apart
>   and cast away their cords from us" (VV. 1-3).

THE BACK STORY

On the surface, Psalm 2 seems to be about a rebellion among the subject peoples who owed allegiance to the king of Israel in Old Testament times. During the flowering of the kingdom under David and Solomon, Israel's power extended far beyond its own borders. At the outset of his reign, reports the biblical writer, "Solomon ruled over all the kingdoms from the Euphrates to the land of the Philistines and to the border of Egypt" (1 KINGS 4:21).

Even when Judah's power and influence were much reduced in

later years following the division of the kingdom, King Jehoshaphat still received tribute from some of his neighbors (2 CHRONICLES 17:10-11). But whenever an overlord died in the ancient world, it was an opportunity for every tribute-paying vassal and ambitious underling to try to gain a little more independence. So in this psalm the scent of rebellion is in the air.

The first thing the new king had to do after his coronation was to assert his authority and reestablish the effective limits of his power. Psalm 2 was probably written to mark the ascent to the throne of a new king of Israel, and the rebelliousness of Israel's subject neighbors (people like the Edomites or Moabites or Philistines) is the back story of this poem.

But of course, that's far from all that is going on here. To say that this psalm is about the dynastic struggles of the house of David is like saying that Hamlet is a story about Danish politics. There is a deeper meaning in the text. The psalm is really about a greater king even than David, a more significant "Anointed One,"—literally, as that Hebrew word says, a *Messiah*.

It is significant that the conspirators in Psalm 2 are said to be plotting first and foremost against the Lord himself. And Christians, from the New Testament onward, have understood the Lord's Anointed to be none other than Jesus—*the* Christ. So the psalmist's description of the attempt to "burst their bonds apart and cast away their cords from us" can also refer to humanity's continual propensity to rebel against the authority of God and of his Christ. The rage of the rulers of the earth in Psalm 2 has its counterpoint in the anger many moderns feel at the thought of any constraints placed upon them "from above." Consider, for example, the feminist pro-abortion slogan, "Don't put your laws on my body," or the firestorm of protest against efforts to legally restrict marriage to its traditional form. Christian cultural observer Ken Myers comments perceptively in his *Mars Hill Audio Journal* about "how many cultural disorders are related to hatred of limits. The aspiration to limitlessness was embedded in the first temptation and original sin . . . and it inspired the founding intellects of modernity." And, we might add, it fuels the hatred of the anti-God crowd today.

Rage Against the Messiah

But however much some may rage against the laws of nature and nature's God, the Lord and his Anointed remain firmly in control. Psalm 2 is quoted often in the New Testament with explicit application to Christ (ACTS 4:25-26; 13:33; HEBREWS 1:5; 5:5). In the book of Acts, for example, we read that the church in Jerusalem turned to this psalm when they were facing persecution from the city's religious authorities.

Peter and John had been called in for examination by the Jewish High Council following the healing of the crippled beggar at the Beautiful Gate outside the temple. It must have been disconcerting to these two leaders of the fledgling Christian church to be hauled before the same tribunal that had condemned their Lord to death just a few weeks (or possibly months) before. But something (Jesus' resurrection) and Someone (the Holy Spirit) had changed these disciples, and Peter boldly confesses the faith: the One whom you condemned and crucified has been raised by God (ACTS 4:10). Salvation is found in him and him alone (V. 12). The chief priests and elders then try to silence Peter and John. They can't very well discredit the power of Jesus' name (V. 10), for the man who had been healed is standing right there in front of them (V. 14). So they try to intimidate the apostles by commanding them "not to speak or teach at all in the name of Jesus" (V. 18). Peter replies by rather blandly suggesting to the Council that they think about whether it is more important to obey God or them, adding that he and John could not (and would not) stop testifying to what they knew.

Upon their release the apostles immediately gathered with the church and reported what had happened. "And when they heard it, they lifted their voices together to God" (V. 24) and prayed these words from Psalm 2:

> Why did the Gentiles rage,
>   and the peoples plot . . . ?
> The kings of the earth set themselves,
>   and the rulers were gathered together,

> against the Lord and against his Anointed.
>
> —*Acts 4:25-26*

These first believers saw in the crucifixion of Jesus the ultimate act of rebellion by the world's rulers against the Lord and his Anointed, Jesus. "For truly in this city there were gathered together against your holy servant Jesus, whom you anointed, both Herod and Pontius Pilate, along with the Gentiles and the peoples of Israel" (v. 27). So it was no wonder to the earliest Christians that they too should face hostility and opposition from the very same people who had plotted against their Lord, and finally brought him to the cross.

Peter and John had testified heroically in the face of the authorities' threats and intimidation. But the danger that the Council's hostility posed to the infant church in Jerusalem was very real. Confronted with this threat, the believers immediately turned to the Lord, and called upon God for help. You might think that they would pray for protection from the authorities, or that they would cry out for the Lord to defeat their enemies. But what they actually asked of God is more remarkable still:

> "And now, Lord," they prayed, "look upon their threats and grant to your servants to continue to speak your word with all boldness" (v. 29).

All they asked for was the courage to go on bearing witness to Jesus when fear for their own safety might urge them to be silent. Years later, when facing possible execution, the apostle Paul prayed along similar lines:

> At the same time, pray also for us, that God may open to us a door for the word, to declare the mystery of Christ, on account of which I am in prison—that I may make it clear, which is how I ought to speak.
>
> —*Colossians 4:3-4*

The early Christians knew they could expect opposition from

the world, and even persecution by political and religious leaders. After all, they had witnessed firsthand what had happened to Jesus, and they remembered his words that a servant is not greater than his master (JOHN 13:16). They were ready to face for Jesus what he had faced for them. But they took comfort in the belief that the God of Jesus would grant courage and strength to them as well in their time of testing. They were confident that the Lord would enable them to be faithful unto death, even as Jesus was. That same assurance can be ours too. We need not fear the plots and threats of the world's anti-God forces, whether they come in the form of state-sponsored or religiously motivated persecution, or in the taunts and jibes of clever atheists. Our God is the Sovereign Lord (ACTS 4:24). He will give us courage and grace to face whatever we must.

"You Are My Son"

Something else in Psalm 2 especially attracted the attention of the New Testament church. After the opening verses where the psalmist refers to the Lord's Anointed, the Messiah himself speaks. "I will tell of the decree," says Christ in verse 7, "The LORD said to me, 'You are my Son; today I have begotten you.'"

This reference identifying God's Anointed One as his Son had an electrifying effect on the writers of the New Testament, as you might well imagine. The apostles saw in this verse a clear prophecy pointing straight to Jesus Christ as both Messiah and Son of God. Peter was the first to make this double identification, in his great confession: "You are the Christ, the Son of the living God" (MATTHEW 16:16). "Blessed are you, Simon," Jesus replies, "for flesh and blood has not revealed this to you, but my Father who is in heaven" (V.17). Is it too much of a stretch to imagine that the Father revealed this truth to Peter not by some visionary flash of inspiration, but rather by opening his eyes to the significance of Psalm 2:7?

The writer of the epistle to the Hebrews quotes this verse as underscoring the superiority of Jesus to even the most glorious created being. "For to which of the angels did God ever say, 'You are my Son, today I have begotten you'?" (HEBREWS 1:5). Paul, both in his missionary preaching (ACTS 13:33) and in his apostolic writing (ROMANS 1:4), relates this declaration to Jesus' resurrection. It was his resurrection from the dead, states the apostle, that fully and finally revealed Jesus in his real nature as the eternal, only begotten Son of God, the true Messiah of whom even the greatest of the anointed kings of Israel were but faint copies.*

So Psalm 2, written originally to glorify the kings of ancient Israel on their coronation day, in its deepest meaning testifies to an infinitely greater King and Son. The most dramatic coronation in history took place not on a throne in a palace in Jerusalem but in an empty tomb just outside the city, when Christ—"the Anointed One"—was once and for all declared to be the Son of God with power.

Be Warned

The second psalm serves not just as a prophetic revelation, though, but as a warning. It offers some serious advice to those scoffers who live as enemies of Jesus and his people. Many today, not just our leading public atheists, have declared their independence from God. While some intellectuals have determined that faith in God is worse than foolish and have set for themselves the task of ridding the world of believers, most secularists are content to simply ignore God and sneer privately at those who trust in him. We needn't be afraid of such folks or worry excessively about their impact. After all, God doesn't need us to defend him from his cultured despisers.

In fact, do you know how God himself responds to those who

---

*The fact that Jesus' resurrection is linked to God's statement to his Son, "Today I have begotten you," does not mean that Jesus *became* the Son of God when he was raised from the dead. Paul asserts in Romans 1:4 that Jesus was declared to be the Son at the resurrection. The verb he uses, *horizo,* can also mean "to appoint." But as K.L. Schmidt explains, "Whether the reference here is to a declaration or an appointment is not a matter of great urgency, since a divine declaration is also a divine appointment. In the light of Acts 10:42 and 17:31, what Christ is now declared or appointed to be is to be equated with what he already is from all eternity by divine ordination" (Geoffrey W. Bromiley, ed., *Theological Dictionary of the New Testament,* abridged, Grand Rapids: Eerdmans, 1985, p. 728.) In orthodox Christian teaching the Father's begetting of the Son is understood to be eternal, without beginning or end. Thus we confess of the Son in the Nicene Creed that he is "begotten, not made, of one substance with the Father." The Resurrection did not make Jesus God's Son; it vindicated his claims to be God's Son, and published that fact to the universe.

attack him? He laughs at them. Look again at Psalm 2: "He who sits in the heavens laughs; the Lord holds them in derision" (V. 4). Now that is a very disconcerting thought. A kindly God, a sympathetic God, a gentle, all-accepting, all-embracing God—that's God as people expect him to be. But a *laughing* God? The image is unsettling, and it's meant to be. This laughter of God against those who set themselves against him is contemptuous laughter. "God . . . from his exalted throne smiles at the manikins and mocks at them."[4] All the rebellious arrogance of tiny little men and women running around shouting that God is dead, God is irrelevant, we have no need of him, we'll destroy all this religious superstition and then make our own future, we'll recreate our very nature, we'll make ourselves immortal—it all strikes God as ludicrous. He laughs such people to scorn.

Which is not to say that any of this is funny. Not at all. It is, rather, terrifying. After God's laughter comes his word of judgment, and what God says to human rebels is deadly serious. "Then he will speak to them in his wrath," declares the psalmist, "and terrify them in his fury" (V. 5). Artur Weiser comments, "A race of pygmies is face to face with a giant."[5] And when this all-holy, all-powerful, infinite God speaks again, it is to bear witness to his Son. All sorts of sophisticated opinion leaders in our society may belittle Jesus Christ and his followers, make fun of them, or even do their best to destroy them. But God's determination cancels theirs. "As for me," says the Almighty, "I have set my King on Zion, my holy hill. . . . I will make the nations your heritage and the ends of the earth your possession" (VV. 6, 8).

In the end, King Jesus will rule over all. All who honor and worship him will be vindicated. All who hate and oppose him will be thrown into confusion, disaster, and eternal ruin. So don't wait: "Kiss the Son, lest he be angry, and you perish in the way. . . . Blessed are all who take refuge in him" (V. 12).

The Bible's testimony to Jesus presents each of us with a fundamental choice to make. If Jesus is the Son of God, the incarnate Second Person of the Holy Trinity, the Anointed One who "was delivered up for our trespasses and raised for our justification"

(ROMANS 4:25), then nothing matters as much as recognizing him and aligning our lives rightly with his.

"Jesus was the only One that ever raised the dead," declares The Misfit in Flannery O'Connor's story *A Good Man Is Hard to Find,*

> and he shouldn't have done it. He thown everything off balance. If He did what He said, then it's nothing for you to do but thow away everything and follow Him, and if He didn't, then it's nothing for you to do but enjoy the few minutes you got left the best way you can—by killing somebody or burning down his house or doing some other meanness to him. No pleasure but meanness.[6]

Flannery O'Connor saw clearly what our modern atheists don't, or at least, what they don't choose to tell us. If there is no God, then anything goes. The only thing to do is to try to find a little pleasure in the few minutes you have left. Though if you happen to find pleasure in gardening, say, and someone else finds pleasure in meanness, there's really nothing you can say. As the Romans so aptly put it, *De gustibus non disputandem est:* you can't argue about tastes.

On the other hand, if Jesus "did what he said," then there is nothing left for us to do but throw everything we have away, and go and follow him. So which is it?

Study Questions

1. With Psalm 2 in the background, how do you make sense of the recent attacks by prominent atheists on belief in God? Why would those critics point to belief in God as a moral failure?

2. Who is being referred to as the conspirators in Psalm 2? Explain how their conspiracy in Psalm 2 translates into rebellion against Christ's authority later on.

3. What can we apply to our lives from the early church's use of Psalm 2 (see ACTS 4:1-31) when it faced persecution from the religious authorities at the time?

4. What event in Jesus' life showed his unassailable claim to be God's Anointed One? Explain how this event served as both a coronation ceremony and a victory celebration.

5. Is it our job to defend God's reputation? Or is God's contemptuous laughter (PSALM 2:4) all that is needed to rout his enemies?

6. True or False. If there is no God, then anything goes. Explain.

Chapter 2

CHRIST OUR SACRIFICE

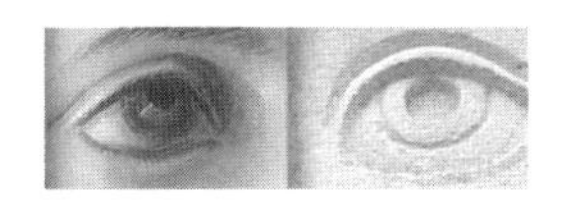

PSALM 40:6-8
HEBREWS 10:1-14

In sacrifice and offering you have not delighted,
but you have given me an open ear.
Burnt offering and sin offering
you have not required.
Then I said, "Behold, I have come;
in the scroll of the book it is written of me:
I delight to do your will, O my God;
your law is within my heart." —*Psalm 40:6-8*

The law is only a shadow of the good things that are coming—not the realities themselves. For this reason it can never, by the same sacrifices repeated endlessly year after year, make perfect those who draw near to worship. If it could, would they not have stopped being offered? For the worshipers would have been cleansed once for all, and would no longer have felt guilty for their sins. But those sacrifices are an annual reminder of sins, because it is impossible for the blood of bulls and goats to take away sins.

Therefore, when Christ came into the world, he said:

"Sacrifice and offering you did not desire,
but a body you prepared for me;
with burnt offerings and sin offerings
you were not pleased.
Then I said, 'Here I am—it is written about me in the scroll—
I have come to do your will, O God.'"

First he said, "Sacrifices and offerings, burnt offerings and sin offerings you did not desire, nor were you pleased with them" (although the law required them to be made). Then he said, "Here I am, I have come to do your will." He sets aside the first to establish the second. And by that will, we have been made holy through the sacrifice of the body of Jesus Christ once for all.

Day after day every priest stands and performs his religious duties; again and again he offers the same sacrifices, which can never take away sins. But when this priest had offered for all time one sacrifice for sins, he sat down at the right hand of God. Since that time he waits for his enemies to be made his footstool, because by one sacrifice he has made perfect forever those who are being made holy.

—Hebrews 10:1-14 NIV

SEVERAL YEARS AGO while traveling in India, I happened to be visiting a Hindu temple just as a priest was offering a sacrifice on behalf of a family of worshipers. I stood a short way off and watched as a small goat was laid on its side on a concrete slab, its legs bound together. The animal, though bleating plaintively, seemed resigned to its fate. The priest's movements were swift and professional as he sure-handedly slit the goat's throat and then dabbed some of its blood on the foreheads of the worshipers.

I remember thinking three things at that moment. The first was that this wasn't how we do church back in Grand Rapids. The second was that such a scene must have been much more like the worship of the Old Testament than our services are. But my third and strongest thought was, "Man, I'm sure glad I don't have to do that." We can all be eternally grateful that such sacrifices are no longer necessary for worshiping God.

"Without the Shedding of Blood . . ."

Yet once upon a time they were. When God instituted the elaborate series of animal sacrifices that were the basis of Israel's daily and annual worship, he was teaching his people a significant lesson. The lesson was that death is required in order for sin to be forgiven and access gained to a holy God. From the very beginning the religion of Israel was bathed in blood. Every morning and evening, first at the tabernacle and later at Solomon's temple, the people approached God by offering up animals in sacrifice. All the great seasonal festivals of the Jewish religion—in particular, the Passover—involved the killing of vast numbers of animals.

That must have made the temple in Jerusalem much more like a slaughterhouse than a quiet cathedral. Its very stones ran red with the life-blood of sacrifices. And throughout the centuries every last one of those offerings, every application of blood to the altar and to the great mercy seat in the Holy of Holies, every single slaughtered lamb and goat and bull, shouted out the truth most clearly stated in the letter to the Hebrews: "Without the shedding of blood there is no forgiveness of sins" (HEBREWS 9:22).

What this verse declares is that the solution to the problem of human sin—forgiveness—requires a payment to be made—death—before it can be offered. The theological term for this is *propitiation.* Propitiation, as J. I. Packer explains, means to avert or pacify God's anger against sin with an offering. "Has the word 'propitiation' any place in your Christianity?" he asks in his classic essay, *The Heart of the Gospel.* "In the faith of the New Testament, it is central."[7] Why is that? Why can't God just forgive people? Why all this emphasis on sacrifice, this insistence on payment? After all, aren't we told to forgive those who wrong us? And if we're supposed to do that, doesn't God do likewise? Isn't it the nature of love simply to forgive? But the very reason we on a personal level can forgive others freely and without regard to justice is because God has personally undertaken to uphold the justice of the universe. When the apostle Paul states that God put Christ forward as a propitiation for sin (ROMANS 3:25), he adds that this "was to show his righteousness . . . so that he might be just and the justifier of the one who has faith in Jesus" (V. 26). We don't just need justification to be saved; we need *just* justification.

God must be just, or he wouldn't be God. He must be just in his justifying. So sin has to be dealt with in a specific way. It can't be ignored or excused or simply covered up. "God requires that his justice be satisfied," declares the Heidelberg Catechism. "Therefore the claims of his justice must be paid in full, either by ourselves or another" (Q. & A. 12).

You know as well as I do that if you have a debt, the only thing that can satisfy it is payment. If you're late with the rent, you don't really need a phone call from your landlord reminding you that it's due. You don't need advice or sympathy from a friend. You don't need credit counseling—well, maybe you do. But what you *most* need right then and there is money!

It's the same with sin. We don't really need to be told to accept ourselves as we are and learn to love ourselves. What we need is someone to pay for our sins. And the payment demanded for sin is nothing less than *death:* "Without the *shedding of blood* there is no forgiveness of sins," says Hebrews 9:22.

What Kind of Sacrifice?

This truth lies behind the whole Old Testament system of religion. The first great lesson of Old Testament worship is that the payment for sin must be death. The second is that God has provided a substitute to die instead of us. Herein lies the great difference between biblical religion and paganism. Pagans believed their gods had to be propitiated with sacrifices, and so they offered them– the bigger, the better. The pagan gods were capricious, touchy, just as likely to do you harm as good, needing to be carefully handled and constantly placated.

The God of the Bible is gracious and merciful in his very essence (EXODUS 33:18-19). We don't propitiate him; indeed, we can't. He does the propitiating for us, by offering a substitute on our behalf. For centuries this substitute was an animal, a sheep or a goat or a bull. But those sacrifices were really only object lessons—substitutes for the real Substitute—because no mere animal's life could ever be precious enough to atone for human wrong-doing. "Because," declares the writer to the Hebrews, "it is impossible for the blood of bulls and goats to take away sins" (HEBREWS 10:4).

So what kind of sacrifice does God really require? The answer to that question is revealed in a remarkable way in Psalm 40, as read through the lens of the book of Hebrews. Despite numerous commands of God's law requiring animal sacrifices in worship and the detailed regulations governing these rituals (for example, in the book of Leviticus), the Old Testament also has another perspective on these offerings. When Psalm 40 talks about sacrifices, it seems to dismiss their importance. The psalmist writes,

> In sacrifice and offering you have not delighted,
> but you have given me an open ear.
> Burnt offering and sin offering
> you have not required.
> Then I said, "Behold, I have come;
> in the scroll of the book it is written of me:
> I delight to do your will, O my God;
> your law is within my heart" (VV. 6-8).

Psalm 40 is called a Psalm of David, and his words here echo another passage from one of the greatest of his psalms, Psalm 51.

> You will not delight in sacrifice, or I would give it;
> you will not be pleased with a burnt offering.
> The sacrifices of God are a broken spirit;
> A broken and contrite heart, O God,
> you will not despise (VV. 16-17).

Or consider this passage from the previous psalm, Psalm 50. The Lord asks,

> Do I eat the flesh of bulls
> or drink the blood of goats? (V. 13).

And then he commands,

> Offer to God a sacrifice of thanksgiving,
> and perform your vows to the Most High,
> and call upon me in the day of trouble;
> I will deliver you and you shall glorify me (VV. 14-15).

All these verses are underscoring the fact that outward sacrifices alone are not enough to please the Lord. What God wants even more than our offerings is the inward sacrifice of repentance, humility, and gratitude. In other words, our attitude counts as much as the quality of our gifts—or more so. And so does our conduct. David goes on to say this in Psalm 40: "I delight to do your will, O my God; your law is within my heart" (V. 8). In addition to our contrite, thankful worship, God is looking for our obedience. As the prophet Micah famously put it, we could give herds of animals and rivers of oil in sacrifice, we could even offer up our own children, but what the Lord really requires of us is "to do justice, and to love kindness, and to walk humbly with [our] God" (MICAH 6:8). Without sincerity our sacrifices are meaningless to God; without obedience, they are downright abhorrent to him.

But that does not make them unnecessary. This is an important point. Many people read a passage like Micah 6:8 and think that the only thing that matters to God is living a moral life. It doesn't matter what you believe as long as you are sincere. It doesn't matter which religion you follow as long as you are kind and tolerant and don't do anything to hurt anyone. Isn't this all God really cares about? But just because the hypocrisy of a worshiper could render his sacrifices null and void, that doesn't mean they could be dispensed with. When David says that the Lord does not delight in sacrifice or require burnt offerings or sin offerings, he is using hyperbole. He's exaggerating in order to stress the importance of both right attitude and right living on the part of every true worshiper of God. Make no mistake: these things are crucial. For our worship to be pleasing to God we must be both inwardly engaged and outwardly obedient. But the truth revealed in God's law remains eternally valid: without the shedding of blood there can be no forgiveness. A sacrifice for sin must still be offered.

The True Sacrifice

We can only understand what this whole system is really about when we turn to the New Testament. We learn there what God always had in mind in instituting all those animal sacrifices. In the tenth chapter of the book of Hebrews the writer quotes the exact verses from Psalm 40 that we have been considering, but with some significant differences. First, he follows the Septuagint, the ancient Greek translation of the Hebrew scriptures, in the second part of Psalm 40:6: "a body you have prepared for me." Then the writer puts these words into the mouth of Christ. "Consequently," he states, "when *Christ* came into the world, *he* said,"

> "Sacrifices and offerings you have not desired,
> but a body you have prepared for me;
> in burnt offerings and sin offerings
> you have taken no pleasure.
> Then I said, 'Behold, I have come to do your will, O God,
> as it is written of me in the scroll of the book.'"
>
> —*Hebrews 10:5-7*

So Jesus, not David, is the speaker who makes these statements; he is the subject to whom the words "me" and "I" in these verses refer. That is to say, this psalm (and, as the psalm affirms, the whole of the Hebrew scriptures) is really all about Christ. It is of him that poets and prophets and sages wrote "in the scroll of the book." He is the one, truly, who has "come to do your will, O God." And because of his perfect obedience, Jesus—the only person who doesn't need a sacrifice for sin—becomes the only person able to make that sacrifice. Hebrews 10:9 states that Christ "sets aside the first" (the sacrificial system of the Old Testament) "to establish the second" (his obedience to God's will, culminating in his becoming obedient even to death on a cross.) The body that will be offered as *the* atoning sacrifice for the sin of the world will not be that of a goat or a sheep or a bull. It will be the body that God prepared for Christ—for himself—when he took upon himself our nature in order to become our sacrifice.

The entire Old Testament points to the ultimate sacrifice finally offered by Jesus Christ. All of that temple ritual was only a sort of shadow version (HEBREWS 10:1) of the actual drama of redemption that took place when Jesus sacrificed his own body on the cross, once and for all, for the sins of the world (1 JOHN 2:2). So, adds the writer, "we have been made holy through the sacrifice of the body of Jesus Christ once for all . . . because by one sacrifice he has made perfect forever those who are being made holy" (HEBREWS 10:10-14, NIV). Christ is our sacrifice: "Behold, the Lamb of God, who takes away the sin of the world" (JOHN 1:29).

Strong Reactions

People tend to react strongly to the idea that Christ is the sacrifice for our sins. For many, the reaction is strongly negative. In our day the doctrine of Christ's death as an atoning sacrifice for our sin—what J. I. Packer calls "the best part of the best news the world has ever heard"—has often come in for heavy criticism, sometimes by its supposed friends. "Penal substitution," which is the shorthand term summing up this understanding of what happened on the cross, is referred to as a "theory"* of the atonement that ought to be dismissed as antiquated. Liberal Christians have always disliked

*John Stott suggests that "theory" is not the appropriate term for this doctrine. "My contention is that substitution is not a further 'theory' or 'image' to be set alongside the others [i.e., explanations of the atonement], but rather the foundation of them all, without which each lacks cogency" (*The Cross of Christ*, Downers Grove: InterVarsity Press, 2006, p. 168.)

this doctrine. To them it stinks of savagery and blood-lust; "divine child abuse," some have called it. "Immoral," "unjust," "an insult to God's loving character" are some of the terms used. Packer's response is on the mark.

> Since all this (the atonement) was planned by the holy Three (the Trinity) in their eternal solidarity of mutual love and since the Father's central purpose in it all was and is to glorify and exalt the Son as Savior and Head of a new humanity, smarty-pants notions like "divine child abuse" as a comment on the cross are supremely silly and as irreverent and wrong as they possibly could be.[8]

Unfortunately, today some evangelical voices have joined the chorus of propitiation's critics. The idea of penal substitution seems to be especially uncongenial to postmodern and "emergent" Christians. It is fair to say that there is now a strong, widespread tendency among even supposedly evangelical Christians to downplay the sacrificial (Christ's death as an offering for sin to pacify the wrath of God) and substitutionary (Christ taking our place to die in our stead) nature of the death of Christ—if not to reject these things altogether.

But there is an equally strong reaction in those of us who hold these truths as the very heart of the gospel. To us who have a deep sense of the dreadful seriousness of sin, who feel the crippling extent of our own depravity, who tremble at the terrible holiness of God, who recognize the just wrath against evil that is the complement in God's character to the great goodness of his love; above all, to us who believe this is Scripture's clear teaching, Christ's sacrificial death means everything. The words of J. I. Packer quoted above are from the introduction to a new collection of essays in defense of the historic understanding of the New Testament's teaching about the atonement. Packer writes,

> An evangelical theologian, dying, cabled a colleague: "I am so thankful for the active obedience [righteousness] of Christ.

No hope without it." As I grow old I want to tell everyone who will listen: "I am so thankful for the penal substitutionary death of Christ. No hope without it."[9]

"Nothing in My Hand I Bring"

What then? Well, the doctrine of penal substitution has some very important practical implications. First among them is that understanding and believing in this doctrine is the key to having personal assurance of our forgiveness and acceptance by God. The writer of Hebrews puts special emphasis on the finality of Christ's sacrifice.

> Day after day every priest stands and performs his religious duties; again and again he offers the same sacrifices, which can never take away sins. But when this priest had offered for all time one sacrifice for sins, he sat down at the right hand of God.
>
> —*Hebrews 10:11-12, NIV*

Because Christ has made the once-for-all offering for sin, sins are completely and forever forgiven for all who are "in Christ," to use a favorite Pauline phrase. Christ's sacrificial work is finished. That's why he is seated in heaven (V. 12). Hebrews also quotes Jeremiah 31:34: "I will remember their sin no more," and adds, "Where there is forgiveness of these, there is no longer any offering for sin" (HEBREWS 10:18).

This biblical emphasis on the finished redemptive work of Christ on the cross is what led the Reformers to reject the entire penitential system of the medieval Catholic Church. That system centered on the 'sacrifice' of the Mass, where the priest re-enacted Christ's sacrifice and made its grace available to those who received Christ's body in the form of bread. It demanded that people who confessed their sins perform various acts of penance to help expiate their guilt. It stressed the terrors and pain of Purgatory, where sinners would continue to suffer after death until they were finally cleansed from their sins—or until the Church, after a suitable contribution from the sinner's family, issued an indulgence that lopped some time off the sentence. To the Reformers this system represented a gross perversion of the heart of the gospel, a demeaning of the finished work of Christ, an illegitimate expansion of the Church's authority, and a needless burdening of the Christian's conscience.

"We have been sanctified (Greek *hegiasmenoi esmen,* in the perfect tense) through the offering of the body of Jesus Christ once for all" (V. 10). This is Hebrews' way of stating the Pauline doctrine of justification by faith in Christ's propitiatory sacrifice (ROMANS 3:21-25). It means our sins are forgiven and our guilt is gone forever. Nothing more to do, no need for us to pay—as if we could. All we need do, says the Heidelberg Catechism, "is to accept the gift of God with a believing heart" (Q. & A. 60). And so, declares one of the classics of Calvinist hymnody,

> Not the labors of my hands
> Can fulfill thy law's demands;
> Could my zeal no respite know,
> Could my tears forever flow,
> All for sin could not atone;
> Thou must save, and thou alone.
>
> Nothing in my hand I bring,
> Simply to thy cross I cling;
> Naked, come to thee for dress,
> Helpless, look to thee for grace;
> Foul, I to the Fountain fly;
> Wash me, Savior, or I die.
>
> —*Augustus M. Toplady, 1776*

Michael Wilcock offers this summary of the message of Psalm 40 as read through the lens of Hebrews. He also well expresses the assurance of faith that comes from believing in Christ our sacrifice.

There is nothing more deeply ingrained in the human heart

than the desire to get into God's good books by offering sacrifices, even by offering obedience, *of one's own.* Psalm 40:6-8, understood in Christian terms, sounds the death knell for all attempts to make oneself right with God and fit for heaven. Out of every such *slimy pit, out of the mud and mire,* he will lift the soul that abandons these hopeless efforts and instead looks eagerly for the blessings that flow from the obedience and sacrifice of Christ.[10]

Living Sacrifices

But there's more, as the infomercials like to say. One of the major objections to the doctrine of the atonement as I have been describing it is that it makes people morally careless. After all, if you're saved by faith alone, and all your sins are forgiven once and for all only because of Christ's sacrifice, why do anything about them yourself? Why worry about striving for personal holiness or working for social justice? Why not just relax and enjoy yourself? That argument is as old as the gospel itself. Paul is responding to it in Romans 6:1-2 when he asks, "Are we to continue in sin that grace may abound? By no means! How can we who died to sin still live in it?" The simple truth is that the gospel of the cross not only deals once for all with our sin and guilt, it also transforms our lives.

The writer to the Hebrews repeats in chapter 10, verse 14, the verb he used in verse 10, a form of *hagiazo,* meaning "sanctify," or "make holy." But he does so with a significant difference. Whereas in verse 10 the verb's tense is perfect, referring to a completed action ("we have been sanctified, made holy") in verse 14 it is in the present tense. "For by a single offering he has perfected for all time those who *are being sanctified.*" Through faith we are made perfect in God's sight—justified—as our sins are completely covered by the sacrificial blood of Christ. But faith also changes us, setting us on the way of ongoing sanctification by which we actually overcome sin and are conformed to the likeness of Christ. His sacrifice becomes our model. With nothing left to pay, we are set free to spend our lives lavishly in service to others. Love for Christ and gratitude for the mercies of God motivate us to offer ourselves as living sacrifices, in conformity to the will of God (ROMANS 12:1-2), not to earn forgiveness but because we have been fully forgiven.

This kind of sacrificial love is what makes Christians—when they are living up to their faith—stand out in a self-seeking world. One great example of this is related by the early church historian Eusibius. Beginning in A.D. 250 and continuing for the next 15 years, a terrible plague swept the Roman Empire. Eusebius, writing two generations later, quotes from a letter of Dionysius, Bishop of Alexandria, that describes the behavior of the Christians in his city during the epidemic.

> Most of our brethren showed love and loyalty in not sparing themselves while helping one another, tending to the sick with no thought of danger and gladly departing this life with them after becoming infected with their disease. Many who nursed others to health died themselves, thus transferring their death to themselves. The best of our own brothers lost their lives in this way—some presbyters, deacons, and laymen—a form of death based on strong faith and piety that seems in every way equal to martyrdom. They would also take up the bodies of the saints, close their eyes, shut their mouths, and carry them on their shoulders. They would embrace them, wash and dress them in burial clothes, and soon receive the same services themselves.
>
> The heathen were the exact opposite. They pushed away those with the first signs of the disease and fled from their dearest. They even threw them half dead into the roads and treated unburied corpses like refuse in hopes of avoiding the plague of death, which for all their efforts, was difficult to escape.[11]

How should I respond to the truth that Christ has fully paid for all my sins with his precious blood? I should accept his sacrifice for me, trust in it, glory in it, proclaim it as the gospel—and then live it out in my own sacrificial living for others.

Study Questions

1. Since God is Almighty, he could just forgive everybody's sins if he wanted to, right? When people say that God's justice had to be satisfied with a perfect sacrifice, it makes me wonder whether God was limited or constrained in some way. Can God be limited in any way?

2. Why do the modern critics of penal substitution (the view that Christ's shed blood is what pacifies the Father's righteous wrath against sin) think this doctrine is immoral and unjust?

3. What role does the doctrine of penal substitution play in having personal assurance of forgiveness and acceptance by God?

4. Why do I still feel guilt and shame for the sins I commit if Christ has paid my sin debt in full?

5. If we can't earn forgiveness, why do we have to be penitent to receive forgiveness?

6. If we are to be grateful for what God has done for us on the cross, shouldn't we spend a little more time reflecting on our own sinfulness? What do you think?

Chapter 3

Christ the Savior

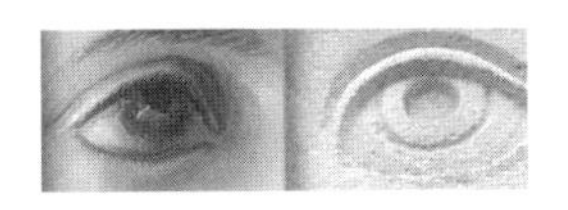

PSALM 22
MATTHEW 27:46

My God, my God, why have you forsaken me?
Why are you so far from saving me, from the words of
    my groaning?
O my God, I cry by day, but you do not answer,
    and by night, but I find no rest.

Yet you are holy,
    enthroned on the praises of Israel.
In you our fathers trusted;
    they trusted, and you delivered them.
To you they cried and were rescued;
    in you they trusted and were not put to shame.

But I am a worm and not a man,
    scorned by mankind and despised by the people.
All who see me mock me;
    they make mouths at me; they wag their heads;
"He trusts in the LORD; let him deliver him;
    let him rescue him, for he delights in him!"

I am poured out like water,
    and all my bones are out of joint;
my heart is like wax;
    it is melted within my breast;
my strength is dried up like a potsherd,
    and my tongue sticks to my jaws;
    you lay me in the dust of death.

For dogs encompass me;
    a company of evildoers encircles me;
they have pierced my hands and feet—I can count all my bones—they stare and gloat over me; they divide my garments among them,
    and for my clothing they cast lots.

—Psalm 22:1-8, 14-18

And about the ninth hour Jesus cried out with a loud voice, saying, "Eli, Eli, lema sabachthani?" that is, "My God, my God, why have you forsaken me?"

—Matthew 27:46

PEOPLE, including very smart people, can get things amazingly wrong. Some years ago *TIME* magazine ran a piece entitled "The Past, Imperfect." It was a series of quotations from eminent persons commenting upon new inventions of the day.

"This 'telephone' has too many shortcomings to be seriously considered as a means of communication. The device is inherently of no value to us."
(From a Western Union internal memo in 1876, in response to Alexander Graham Bell's offer to sell them the rights to his new invention. He went on to found AT&T. Western Union went on to specialize in wiring money orders.)

"Heavier-than-air flying machines are impossible."

(Lord Kelvin, one of the most respected of all British scientists and President of the Royal Society (of Science), in 1895. Wilbur and Orville were already tinkering in their bicycle shop at the time.)

"Everything that can be invented has been invented."
(Charles H. Duell, Commissioner of the U.S. Patent Office, on his reason for suggesting in 1899 that the office be closed down.)

"The wireless music box has no imaginable commercial value. Who would pay for a message sent to nobody in particular?"
(The response to David Sarnoff, Chairman of the RCA Corporation and later of NBC, from his associates when he urged that they invest in radio in the 1920s.)

"I think there is a world market for maybe five computers."
(Thomas Watson, Chairman of IBM, 1943.)

People got it amazingly wrong about Jesus too. While almost everyone alive today at the very least respects and honors Jesus as one of the world's most sublime religious teachers, in his own day many—if not most—people scorned and ridiculed him. It was as the prophecies had foretold:

But I am a worm and not a man,
    scorned by mankind and despised by the people.
All who see me mock me;
    they make mouths at me; they wag their heads . . . .

—Psalm 22:6-7

He was despised and rejected by men;
    a man of sorrows, and acquainted with grief;
and as one from whom men hide their faces
    he was despised, and we esteemed him not.

Surely he has borne our griefs

> and carried our sorrows;
> yet we esteemed him stricken,
> smitten by God, and afflicted.
>
> —*Isaiah 53:3-4*

Jesus—mocked as he suffered (and suffered for the very ones who mocked), despised as a criminal, rejected as a God-cursed sinner; how wrong can people be?

The Suffering Savior

No psalm points as clearly to the Savior or speaks as poignantly of his sufferings as does Psalm 22. When we read the words of this psalm it is as though we have left the Old Testament and find ourselves in the Gospels, reading their eyewitness description of Jesus' crucifixion. Here is the taunting of the crowd on Golgotha.

> All who see me mock me;
> they make mouths at me; they wag their heads;
> "He trusts in the Lord; let him deliver him;
> let him rescue him, for he delights in him!" (vv. 7-8).

Here's the physical torment of a crucified man, the man who called out, "I thirst."

> I am poured out like water,
> and all my bones are out of joint;
> my heart is like wax;
> it is melted within my breast;
> my strength is dried up like a potsherd,
> and my tongue sticks to my jaws;
> you lay me in the dust of death (vv. 14-15).

Here is the suffering—emotional as well as physical—of a man who is betrayed and abandoned to his enemies by those closest to him, and then nailed to a Roman cross by heartless soldiers.

> For dogs encompass me;
> a company of evildoers encircles me;
> they have pierced my hands and feet
> —I can count all my bones—
> they stare and gloat over me (VV. 16-17).

Finally, here is the victim whose only possession, a seamless robe, is tossed for by his executioners.

> They divide my garments among them,
> and for my clothing they cast lots (V. 18).

All these verses, which describe in picture-perfect detail the passion of Jesus Christ, are taken verbatim from Psalm 22. It makes me wonder how anyone could read this psalm and fail to see Jesus Christ described there. Perhaps it was a passage such as Psalm 22 that the apostle had in mind when he spoke of those whose minds and hearts are veiled when they read the Old Testament, so that they fail to recognize Jesus there (2 CORINTHIANS 3:14-15; 4:3-4).

But none of the texts I have quoted speaks to the full depth of Christ's suffering on the cross. They touch upon various details of the physical and psychological abuse that Jesus had to take from the soldiers and crowd on Good Friday. But they do not describe the source of his deepest pain. For that we must turn to another verse from the psalm, the most haunting one of all, the words Jesus himself quoted as he hung on the cross while a noonday darkness fell on Golgotha: *My God, my God, why have you forsaken me?*

The God-Forsaken God

So powerful was the impression those terrible words from Psalm 22:1 made upon those of Jesus' followers who heard them as they stood by the cross that years later when they wrote down what happened, they transcribed them exactly as Jesus spoke them, preserving even the sound of the original Aramaic in which Jesus spoke: *Eli, Eli, lema sabachtani . . . My God, my God, why have you forsaken me?* (MATTHEW 27:46; cf. MARK 15:34)

But what do these words mean? This cry from the darkness has long troubled many people. Can Jesus' cry of desertion really mean what it seems to? God would never desert or abandon his righteous Son, would he? *Could* God even do that? Jesus, as every Christian believes, was actually God himself, God in human form. How can God desert himself? How could the eternal unity of the Trinity be ruptured? How is it possible for God to forsake God?

Theologians, preachers, and commentators have long struggled to explain the words that express the very heart of Christ's suffering on the cross. They are what the biblical scholar F. F. Bruce called "the hardest of Jesus' hard sayings."

People have made repeated attempts to soften what Jesus seems to be expressing here. Some have argued that his cry of dereliction doesn't really mean what it sounds like. God could not, and would not, abandon his Son. So there are various alternate explanations: Perhaps Christ is merely expressing his feelings of abandonment here, not the reality. Or maybe he is wrestling with his doubt, as so many of us do when we are in terrible pain, but nevertheless God is still there all the time. Some have suggested that Jesus actually recited not just the beginning but the whole of Psalm 22, including the last verses which end on a note of trust and hope, thus turning the cry of dereliction upside down and making it a confession of faith.

But I think we have to be careful about any attempts to psychologize Christ on the cross, or to make his terrible words of abandonment mean something other than what they plainly state. After all, we can't enter into Jesus' mind. We can't know what was going on there. We don't have the right to judge him against the standard of ourselves. It's a serious mistake to project onto him our weaknesses and doubts and fears. It is false logic to argue that because *my* faith might have been broken on the cross, and Jesus is human like me, therefore *his* faith must have been broken too. No. We cannot claim to understand Christ's experience better than he himself did. We must take Jesus' words at face value, as expressing a true reality. He said what he did because in one infinite, earthshaking, awful moment, God the Father really had turned his back on the Son, and abandoned him. As John Stott writes:

> So then an actual and dreadful separation took place between the Father and the Son; it was voluntarily accepted by both the Father and the Son; it was due to our sins and their just reward; and Jesus expressed this horror of great darkness, this God-forsakenness, by quoting the only verse of Scripture which accurately described it, and which he had perfectly fulfilled.[12]

The Ultimate Penalty

It is not possible to understand the depth of the meaning of the cross of Jesus Christ without coming to grips with the mystery of these words: "My God, my God, why have you forsaken me?" They point us to the ultimate nature of Christ's suffering. It was not just physical (the wounds, the weariness, the thirst), or psychological (the taunting of the crowd, the desertion by his friends). Christ's deepest suffering was spiritual. Before he died physically, he died spiritually. He passed through the dreadful experience of being cut off from God, separated from the God who is the source of all life and light. He, who from all eternity had never known an instant without the conscious delight of perfect fellowship with God the Father, suffered the ultimate death, death in the final sense—the utter desolation of banishment from the presence of the God of love. He was cut off from God. His suffering at that moment was, in some way beyond our understanding, infinite.

> *O all ye who pass by, behold and see;*
> Man stole the fruit, but I must climb the tree;
> The tree of life to all, but only me:
> Was ever grief like mine?
>
> Lo, here I hang, charg'd with a world of sin,
> the greater world o' th' two; for that came in
> by words, but this by sorrow I must win:
> Was ever grief like mine?

> Such sorrow, as if sinful man could feel,
> Or feel his part, he would not cease to kneel
> Till all were melted, though he were all steel:
> Was ever grief like mine?
>
> But, *O my God, my God!* why leav'st thou me,
> The son, in whom thou dost delight to be?
> *My God, my God—*
> Never was grief like mine.
>
> —*George Herbert,* The Sacrifice

That does seem incredible: the God-forsaken God, Jesus Christ. It wasn't just as a man that Jesus suffered divine abandonment. Christian orthodoxy holds that when God became incarnate his two natures, divine and human, though distinct, were inseparably united in the one Person of Jesus. So whatever happened to Jesus happened to him as God, as well as man. This mystery is beyond our grasp, yet in it lies our salvation. Christ the Savior so closely identified with sinners on the cross, that the Bible says, "God made him to be sin for us" (2 CORINTHIANS 5:21, NIV). He took our place and allowed sin's ultimate punishment to fall upon himself. He absorbed all of God's judgment and wrath against sin, and was cut off from him as we forever should have been.

God, you know, always takes sin seriously. Have you ever had something like this happen? Some friends were visiting in our home when their little boy accidently dropped a dish and it smashed on the floor. "It's okay, Dave," he said to me brightly. "You can just buy another one." Easy for him to say. He didn't have to pay for it! There is something at once childish and presumptuous about those who in effect say to God of their sins, "That's okay, you can just forgive them!" We sometimes make light of sin or try to laugh it off. But God never does, because he has to pay for it.

The truth, wonderful beyond the power of words to express, is that God has done just that. He has paid for our sin, paid in full. There is nothing left for us to contribute; "Jesus paid it all," as the song says. His cry of desertion and abandonment on the cross alerts us to the moment when he made this full and final payment. It reveals the lowest depths to which he went—because in order to save us Jesus literally went to hell. There was hell for him so that there wouldn't have to be hell for those who believe in him.

Forsaken, So We Can Be Accepted

I don't think it's possible for anyone to take the gospel as seriously as they should unless they also take seriously the reality of hell. Hell is not everlasting flames or outer darkness; those are merely biblical images that attempt to convey the inconceivable anguish of eternal judgment. The reality of hell is permanent separation, final and forever exclusion, from the presence of God, the source of all good. I know of no words that can convey the awfulness of this reality, but John Donne's perhaps come closest:

> When we have given those words by which hell is expressed in the scriptures the heaviest significations . . . when all is done, the hell of hells, the torment of torments is the everlasting absence of God, and the everlasting impossibility of returning to his presence . . . . To fall out of the hands of the living God is a horror beyond our expression, beyond our imagination . . . . That that God should lose and frustrate all his own purposes and practises upon me, and leave me, and cast me away as though I had cost him nothing, that this God at last should let this soul go away as a smoke, as a vapor, as a bubble, and that then this soul cannot be a smoke, nor a vapor, nor a bubble, but must lie in darkness as long as the Lord of light is light itself, and never a spark of that light reach to my soul; what Tophet is not Paradise, what Brimstone is not Amber, what gnashing is not a comfort, what gnawing of the worm is not a tickling, what torment is not a marriage bed to this damnation, to be secluded eternally, eternally, eternally from the sight of God?[13]

Jesus once told one of his critics that those who have been forgiven much, love much. We might add that those who have been saved from much, and who see clearly how much their salvation cost their Savior, will love even more. The old communion liturgy of the Reformed Church reminded believers as they approached the Lord's Table of the full extent of what Christ has done for them. In the Lord's Supper we remember:

> that our Lord Jesus Christ . . . was sent of the Father into the world: that He assumed our flesh and blood: that He bore for us the wrath of God, under which we should have perished everlastingly . . . that He fulfilled for us all obedience to the divine law . . . . He was bound that we might be freed . . . . He . . . suffered . . . reproaches, that we might never be confounded . . . . He, although innocent, was condemned to death, that we might be acquitted at the judgment-seat of God . . . . He . . . took upon Himself the curse due to us, that He might fill us with His blessings . . . . He humbled Himself unto the deepest reproach and pains of hell . . . on the tree of the cross, when he cried out with a loud voice, *"My God, My God! Why hast thou forsaken me?"* that we might be accepted of God, and never be forsaken of Him . . . .
>
> —*Liturgy of the Reformed Church in America, 1882*

Christ was forsaken that we might be accepted. That's the gospel.

People can and do abandon us. Even those whom we love the most, and who most love us, will someday leave us—or we will leave them. It will happen through death, if not before. But God never fails or abandons those who are his own. "He has said, 'I will never leave you nor forsake you'" (HEBREWS 13:5). If you believe in Jesus Christ the Savior, if you have put your faith in him, then this promise is yours. Because Christ the Savior was once abandoned by God, you never will be.

Can you ever thank him enough?

Study Questions

1. What was Jesus' deepest source of pain? How should we take his haunting words of dereliction in Matthew 27:46?

2. What do Jesus' words of abandonment from his Father (MATTHEW 27:46) communicate about the gravity of our sin?

3. What are some of the reasons that Christians try to soften the Father's abandonment of his Son on the cross? What are some of the unintended theological consequences of that move?

4. What is hell? Why is it so utterly terrible?

5. Explain how God's abandonment of his Son on the cross means that those in Christ will always be found. See Hebrews 13:5.

Chapter 4

CHRIST THE VICTOR

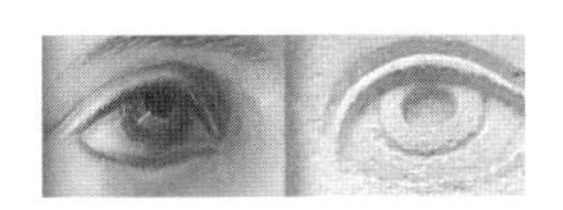

PSALM 16
ACTS 2:25-32

Preserve me, O God, for in you I take refuge.
I say to the LORD, "You are my Lord; I have no good apart
    from you."
As for the saints in the land, they are the excellent ones,
    in whom is all my delight.
The sorrows of those who run after another god shall multiply;
    their drink offerings of blood I will not pour out
    or take their names on my lips.
The LORD is my chosen portion and my cup;
    you hold my lot.
The lines have fallen for me in pleasant places;
    indeed, I have a beautiful inheritance.
I bless the LORD who gives me counsel;
    in the night also my heart instructs me.
I have set the LORD always before me;
    because he is at my right hand, I shall not be shaken.
Therefore my heart is glad, and my whole being rejoices;
    my flesh also dwells secure.
For you will not abandon my soul to Sheol,
    or let your holy one see corruption.

> You make known to me the path of life;
> in your presence there is fullness of joy;
> at your right hand are pleasures forevermore.
>
> —*Psalm 16*

> Brothers, I may say to you with confidence about the patriarch David that he both died and was buried, and his tomb is with us to this day. Being therefore a prophet, and knowing that God had sworn with an oath to him that he would set one of his descendants on his throne, he foresaw and spoke about the resurrection of the Christ, that he was not abandoned to Hades, nor did his flesh see corruption. This Jesus God raised up, and of that we all are witnesses.
>
> —*Acts 2:29-32*

MOST MORNINGS I like to skim the headlines of the *New York Times* online as part of my "start-of-the-day" routine. One item I always look for is a recurring feature in the *Times* real estate section. It's an article entitled, "What You Get For $____" with an amount filled in. So on a given day it could be "What You Get for $1 Million," or "What You Get for $7 Million," or "$12 Million"—or whatever. (The amounts have nose-dived since the recession.) The way the feature works online is that you put your cursor over the slideshow, click your mouse button, and scroll through a series of gorgeous photos of three different properties in different parts of the country, all of which are listed on the market at the given price. After enjoying a number of these displays, I have come to one definite conclusion: if you're wealthy enough, you can have a really nice home in a really beautiful place. Big surprise!

Pleasant Places

In our society property values are determined by market forces, which is why rich folks own all the view lots and waterfront property. It was different in the Bible. When Israel conquered the Promised Land, God directed that the territory should be divided and then distributed to the various tribes and clans by lot. Eight and a half chapters of the book of Joshua describe this process, in rather more detail than perhaps we would have asked for. But this is the background to Psalm16—the song of a happy man. For him, life is good: "The lines have fallen for me in pleasant places; indeed, I have a beautiful inheritance" (V. 6). In other words, this man had struck it rich in the territorial sweepstakes. And because of the law of the Year of Jubilee (LEVITICUS 25), the psalmist's "beautiful inheritance" could never be permanently lost to him and his descendents.

But before we start to picture this man as the Old Testament equivalent of a mega-millions lottery winner ecstatic over his good fortune, we need to look at the text more closely. The psalm begins with a cry for help. "Preserve me, O God, for in you I take refuge" (V. 1). It proceeds to a confession of faith. "I say to the Lord, 'You are my Lord; I have no good apart from you'" (V. 2). Life is good for the psalmist because the Lord is his true good. It's not his flocks and his fields—the view from his deck, or the stuff in his garage—that made this man happy. It was a choice he had made. His real inheritance wasn't the "pleasant places" allotted to his family in the land of Canaan. His real inheritance was God; "The Lord is my chosen portion and my cup" (V. 5).

Because the psalmist knew and loved God, he refused to worship the idols of his culture (V. 14), idols whose names and faces change (*Baal, Mammon, Eros*) but whose essential nature doesn't (*Power, Money, Sex*). Because his whole life was centered on God, the psalmist's security was not affected by things that happened to him: "Because he is at my right hand, I shall not be shaken" (V. 8). So he remained steady in every storm because of his assurance of God's constant presence with him. The psalmist knew almost nothing about the physical world he lived in. (Remember those ancient maps with all the blank spaces marked "*Terra Incognita*"?) But he always knew where he was going: "I have set the Lord always before me." By contrast, people today, armed with GPS-enabled iPhones and dashboard navigation systems, always know exactly where they are on the map. But so many are spiritually lost, aimlessly drifting along. Our society is awash in those who are wondering, Who am I? What is my life about? Why am I so dissatisfied? What would make me happy?

This ancient man of faith points us to the answer, an answer that even he could not fully understand. His confession of faith in the saving power and presence of the Lord rises to the pinnacle of Old Testament hope as he contemplates his own future. Somehow he knows that God will not abandon him—neither soul nor body—to death. God would be his true inheritance not only in this life but beyond. In some way transcending his ability to understand or imagine, the psalmist believes that he will be led through death into the presence of the Lord in whom alone eternal life and infinite joy are found. "You make known to me the path of life; in your presence there is fullness of joy; at your right hand are pleasures forevermore" (V. 11).

But how could this happen?

On the Day of Pentecost

Fast-forward several centuries. On a Jewish religious holiday called Pentecost, in about the year A.D. 30, 120 or so of Jesus' followers are gathered together in the city of Jerusalem. They are waiting for something to happen. This little group—a motley collection of working-class folk, fishermen, housewives and the like—isn't quite sure what it is that's supposed to happen, but Jesus had told them to wait there in the city until a special power came upon them. Shortly before 9 o'clock on a Sunday morning, it did.

While the disciples were all praying together in a large upper room, there was an unusual sound, a mighty rushing noise like a powerful wind. Then dancing tongues of fire-like flame appeared above their heads. Both those phenomena were signs of the coming of God's Holy Spirit, the Spirit of Jesus himself, who had been crucified and raised from the dead just seven weeks before. And as this Spirit filled them, Jesus' followers were moved into action.

Rushing out into the open, they began to speak about all the mighty things God had done through Jesus. Because Jerusalem was crowded with pilgrims who had come from all over the Roman Empire for the religious holiday, the disciples soon attracted a large crowd of onlookers. The words they spoke struck the various listeners in that international crowd with astonishment, not only because of what the disciples said, but because they were speaking in each listener's native language.

The crowd was amazed as much by the medium as by the message. "We hear them telling the mighty works of God in our own tongues!" they exclaimed (ACTS 2:11). This was the miracle of the tongues of Pentecost. The Holy Spirit miraculously enabled Jesus' disciples to speak foreign languages that day so they could proclaim to the peoples of the world *in their own languages* the amazing news of the mighty acts of God through Jesus Christ. It's a work we at Words of Hope continue to do today (though it takes us considerably more time, money, and effort than it did for the believers on Pentecost).

Peter Takes the Lead

All during the three years when Jesus' disciples lived and walked with him, Peter was their principal spokesman. Peter was the leader, the talker, the bold, blustery one. Sometimes his confident talk got him into trouble, most notably on the night when Jesus was arrested. Peter, you may recall, turned coward and loudly denied ever knowing Jesus. But on this day of Pentecost, Peter is a changed man. He becomes a fearless spokesman for the Lord Jesus before this huge multitude, a crowd that even included some of the very leaders who had conspired to put Jesus to death, as Peter will not hesitate to tell them to their faces.

As that vast throng of many thousands of curious onlookers gathers around the Holy-Spirit-driven disciples (most likely in the temple court), Peter begins to address them. He tells them the good news that Jesus was God's Anointed One, the Messiah. He rehearses the basic facts of his life, especially his death and resurrection. He reminds the people in plain words of their own complicity in Jesus' crucifixion. And he offers the hope of salvation, forgiveness, and new life in Christ to all who will repent, believe and be baptized.

The main subject of Peter's famous Pentecost sermon is the Lord Jesus Christ himself. Peter's theme is those great acts by which Jesus accomplished salvation for his people, especially his death and resurrection. In the sermon Peter declared that:

> this Jesus, delivered up according to the definite plan and foreknowledge of God, you crucified and killed by the hands of lawless men. God raised him up, loosing the pangs of death, because it was not possible for him to be held by it . . . . This Jesus God raised up, and of that we are all witnesses (ACTS 2:23-24, 32).

The crucifixion of Jesus was a gross perversion of human justice. But at the same time, this terrible sin was used by God according to his predetermined plan as the perfect sacrifice to pay for sins. Nor did God permit Jesus to remain the victim of sin and the captive of death, but he raised him in triumph and glory from the grave to secure eternal life for all who put their trust in Christ.

JESUS AND THE VICTORY OF GOD

A recent book by N. T. Wright is entitled *Jesus and the Victory of God.* That really would make an excellent title for Peter's great Pentecost sermon as well. This victory wasn't just described in the evangelists' Gospels or proclaimed in the apostles' sermons; it was also prophesied in the Old Testament scriptures. When he began to preach Peter didn't simply announce the fact of Jesus' death and resurrection. He grounded those events in the prophetic teaching of the Old Testament. Throughout his Pentecost sermon Peter quotes from the Psalms and the prophets of the Hebrew scriptures. Christian preaching from the very outset takes the form of biblical exposition, or in this instance, of biblical recitation. "We are witnesses of these things," declared Peter on behalf of the other apostles. And so they were. But so also were the Old Testament writers. All of Scripture—the whole Bible from beginning to end—points to Jesus Christ.

The theme of Peter's message can be simply stated: *This is that. This*—Jesus' death, resurrection, exaltation, and outpouring of the Spirit, resulting in the phenomena of the Day of Pentecost—is *that*—what the Old Testament scriptures prophesied would happen in the last days. "You killed Jesus," Peter declares to the crowd with jaw-dropping boldness, "but God raised him up." And then he turns to Psalm 16 for confirmation of this truth. In fact, Peter quotes the entire second half of the psalm (ACTS 2:25-28).

As we have seen, the words of the psalmist (traditionally David, as Peter affirms) testify to his unshakeable confidence that nothing could separate him from the Lord whose presence means life and joy. Even death would not cut David off from God, for the Lord would not abandon his soul to Sheol (the realm of the dead) or let his body decay in the grave. But now comes something interesting. As he quotes Psalm 16 Peter immediately goes on to point out that this promise could not be referring to David himself, at least not then and there. "I may say to you with confidence about . . . David," remarks Peter to the crowd, "that he both died and was buried, and his tomb is with us to this day" (ACTS 2:29). So if, as anyone in Jerusalem could see for themselves, David was still in his tomb with his body turned to dust these past thousand years, what then could the words of this psalm mean? Peter explains:

> Being therefore a prophet, and knowing that God had sworn with an oath to him that he would set one of his descendants on his throne, [David] foresaw and spoke about the resurrection of the Christ, that he was not abandoned to Hades, nor did his flesh see corruption. This Jesus God raised up, and of that we are all witnesses. . . . Let all . . . therefore know for certain that God has made him both Lord and Christ, this Jesus whom you crucified (ACTS 2:30-32, 36).

So the promises of Psalm 16 refer first and foremost to Jesus, and they predict his triumphant resurrection from the grave. The resurrection of Jesus really is the victory of God, and in refusing to abandon Christ's soul to Hades or leave his body to corrupt in the tomb, God is thereby proclaiming Christ the Victor. The Resurrection is Jesus' great vindication. It marks his victory over all his enemies, all who participated in his destruction: the Jerusalem authorities who feared and resented his popularity, the scribes and Pharisees who hated him for his independence, the Romans who saw him as a threat to their power, the crowd who turned on him when he disappointed their expectations.

More importantly, Christ's resurrection proclaims him to be triumphant over the evil spiritual powers, over sin and death and the devil himself. "He is the beginning, the firstborn from the dead" (COLOSSIANS 1:18). He "disarmed the rulers and authorities"—all the forces of darkness—"triumphing over them in [the cross]" (COLOSSIANS 2:15). "The evil world will not win at last," wrote the Scottish theologian P. T. Forsyth, "because it failed to win at the only time it ever could. It is a vanquished world where men play their deviltries. Christ has overcome it. It can make tribulation, but desolation it can never make."[14]

More Good News

"Jesus," writes Frank (age 8), "You must have got a big smile on your face when you found out you was resurrected. I was glad when I heard about it too. Luv, Frank"[15] Well, Frank, I was glad when I heard about it too, because the resurrection proclaims that Christ has won the victory. That is Gospel; Good News. And here's more Good News: Christ shares his victory with us. Because he lives, we too shall live. God's great promise that "in your presence there is fullness of joy and at your right hand are pleasures forevermore" will come true for us in him. Christ is Victor through his resurrection from the dead.

Tucked away on the narrow streets of Old Istanbul stands a building called the Chora Museum. It's actually an ancient church, the Church of the Holy Savior in Chora, as it originally was called.

The walls and ceiling domes of this 14th-century building are adorned with magnificent mosaics and frescoes, making it a treasure house of Byzantine art. One of the masterpieces there is a fresco depicting Christ's descent into hell after his crucifixion, to set free the captive saints of the Old Testament and bring them with him on his triumphant ascent (cf. Ephesians 4:8-10, citing, in yet another example of Christ in the Psalms, Psalm 68:18). In the painting, the triumphant Christ stands on hell's broken doors, with pieces of chain and broken fetters scattered beneath his feet. He holds out his right hand to Adam, and his left to Eve, raising them both from their tombs. Standing behind Adam is King David, first in a long line of saints waiting to join the train as the Lord begins his ascent to glory. In the western church this traditional scene is called "The Harrowing of Hell." But the Greek title for it, painted above the head of Christ the Victor, is *Anastasis,* "Resurrection."

Because Christ, by his resurrection, has defeated every evil power, all of the Bible's good promises will come true for those who know and love him. This includes the promise that he will not abandon us to death. Someday—Anastasis Day—David will be raised from his grave, and his body will be restored to him uncorrupted. And so will yours, if you belong to Christ. "Have no fear, then," counsels St. Athanasius.

> Now that the common Saviour of all has died on our behalf, we who believe in Christ no longer die, as men died afore time, in fulfilment of the threat of the law. That condemnation has come to an end; and now that, by the grace of the resurrection, corruption has been banished and done away, we are loosed from our mortal bodies in God's good time for each, so that we may obtain thereby a better resurrection.[16]

Amen. So be it! Because Christ is the Victor, we will live forever with him in whose presence is fullness of joy. One day we will "obtain a better resurrection." But even now, before that day, death is transformed into life for those who belong to Christ. For us the sting of death, sin, has been drawn, and the threat of the law nullified. Death does not destroy us, it merely translates us to our home in heaven. "There [in heaven] is Christian, thy husband that was," Christianna is told, "with legions more his companions, ever beholding that face that doth minister life to beholders."[17] So fear not, believer!

Jesus lives, and death is now
But my entrance into glory.
Courage, then, my soul, for thou
Hast a crown of life before thee;
Thou shalt find thy hopes were just;
Jesus is the Christian's trust.

—Christian Gellert, tr. by J. D. Lang

Study Questions

1. What is your inheritance? (What do you love the most?) Is it a pleasant place or some other material thing? What about the Lord? Is he your "portion" and your "cup" as the psalmist writes (PSALM 16:5)?

2. What parallels, if any, do you see in the Holy Spirit's gift of equipping believers to speak foreign languages at Pentecost and the modern work of Bible translation?

3. Do you see God's activity in your life as mirroring in a way Peter's experience of being tested, having failed, and then boldly empowered to declare the gospel? We've all been tested, and we all have certainly failed, but have you ever experienced God's power to boldly proclaim the Good News?

4. Unpack the prophetic and theological implications of Peter's simple theme—"This is that"—in his Acts 2 sermon. Why is Psalm 16 so foundational to Peter's sermon?

5. Identify three effects or results of Christ's resurrection from the dead. State why they are important for your own spiritual growth.

6. Did Jesus literally descend into hell to battle the powers of darkness? What is important about this question? What might be lost theologically if Jesus' descent into hell is spiritualized?

Chapter 5

CHRIST THE LORD

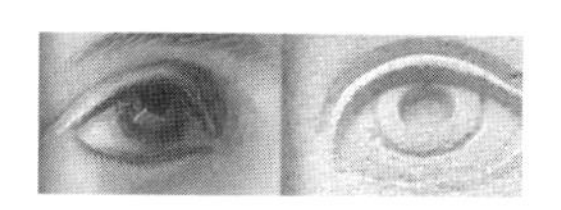

PSALM 110
ACTS 2:33-36

The LORD says to my Lord:
    "Sit at my right hand,
until I make your enemies your footstool."

The LORD sends forth from Zion
    your mighty scepter.
    Rule in the midst of your enemies!
Your people will offer themselves freely
    on the day of your power,
    in holy garments;
from the womb of the morning,
    the dew of your youth will be yours.
The LORD has sworn
    and will not change his mind,
"You are a priest forever
    after the order of Melchizedek."

The Lord is at your right hand;
    he will shatter kings on the day of his wrath.
He will execute judgment among the nations,

filling them with corpses;
he will shatter chiefs
over the wide earth.
He will drink from the brook by the way;
therefore he will lift up his head. *—Psalm 110*

Being therefore exalted at the right hand of God, and having received from the Father the promise of the Holy Spirit, he has poured out this that you yourselves are seeing and hearing. For David did not ascend into the heavens, but he himself says,

"'The Lord said to my Lord, Sit at my right hand,
until I make your enemies your footstool.'

Let all the house of Israel therefore know for certain that God has made him both Lord and Christ, this Jesus whom you crucified."

—Acts 2:33-36

DO YOU HAVE A FAVORITE BIBLE VERSE? It appears that the New Testament apostles did. Their Bible, of course, was limited to the Hebrew scriptures of the Old Testament, while ours includes the 27 books written by the apostles or their disciples. These New Testament writings often quote from different parts of the Old Testament, but there was one verse in particular that drew their attention again and again. It was Psalm 110:1: "The Lord says to my Lord, 'Sit at my right hand, until I make your enemies your footstool.'" In what surely must be a record, this verse is either directly quoted or explicitly referred to no less than 17 times in 12 different books of the New Testament.

Why such interest in a single verse? What is it about this statement that so appealed to the New Testament writers? What meaning or significance did they see in it? Psalm 110:1 is clearly a messianic text, referring not just to a human king of Israel, but to the Messiah, the Anointed One, the Christ. God declares here in the Old Testament both the lordship and enthronement of his Christ. In the New Testament the apostle Peter spoke for all Christians in identifying Jesus as this Lord. Right at the outset, on the very "birthday" of the church, this text becomes the key to understanding the true nature and identity of Jesus of Nazareth. Peter quotes Psalm 110:1 at the heart of his Pentecost sermon. Following his citation of Psalm 16 as a prophecy of Christ's resurrection (see chapter 4 above), Peter declares,

> This Jesus God raised up, and of that we all are witnesses. Being therefore exalted at the right hand of God, and having received from the Father the promise of the Holy Spirit, he has poured out this that you yourselves are seeing and hearing. For David did not ascend into the heavens, but he himself says,
>
> > "The Lord said to my Lord, 'Sit at my right hand,
> > until I make your enemies your footstool.'
>
> Let all the house of Israel therefore know for certain that God has made him both Lord and Christ, this Jesus whom you crucified."
>
> —*Acts 2:32-36*

Peter's transformation here is nothing short of miraculous. The cowardly fisherman who slunk away into the night after denying he even knew Christ now stands in broad daylight and proclaims to the very crowd that killed Jesus that God has reversed their judgment. And from that day to this, all who have responded to this apostolic message with repentance and faith, as 3,000 people did then, have been added to the number of those being saved (c.f. ACTS 2:47).

Jesus Is Lord

The New Testament sees first of all in Psalm 110:1 a declaration of the full identity of Jesus Christ. This text answers the most basic of questions concerning him: Who is Jesus? And it answers it in the most exalted of ways: Jesus is Lord! The Greek word for "Lord" is *Kurios*. Jesus is addressed as *Kurios* many times in the New Testament, in a variety of contexts. The term has different shades of meaning in the Gospels, ranging from polite respect on the lips of a stranger—in which case it simply meant "Sir"—to full-blown worship, as when Thomas falls to his knees before Jesus, crying, "My Lord and my God!" But after the Resurrection there is never any ambiguity about the word. To call Jesus Lord is to acknowledge him as God, plain and simple.

Jesus himself pointed to this understanding of Psalm 110. If you are familiar with the Gospels, you will recall that Jesus' enemies often tried to trap or embarrass him by asking him difficult questions. But on one occasion he turned the tables on his critics by asking them a question of his own, a question that focused on Psalm 110:1.

> . . . while the Pharisees were gathered together, Jesus asked them a question, saying, "What do you think about the Christ? Whose son is he?" They said to him, "The son of David." He said to them, "How is it then that David, in the Spirit, calls him Lord, saying,
>
> > " 'The Lord said to my Lord, Sit at my right hand,
> > until I put your enemies under your feet'?
>
> If then David calls him Lord, how is he his son?" And no one was able to answer him a word, nor from that day did anyone dare to ask him any more questions.
>
> —*Matthew 22:41-46*

Jesus confounded his adversaries by appealing to the riddle at the center of Psalm 110:1. Everyone agreed that the Messiah would be David's descendant, in fulfillment of God's promises to the house of David. But then, asks Jesus, how can David refer to him as "my Lord," and therefore clearly his superior? How can the same person be both the son of David and the Lord of David? The Pharisees were silenced by a question they couldn't answer. But the answer is given to us later in the New Testament by the apostle Paul. Paul writes in Romans 1 that he has been called by God to the service of the gospel, which is the message concerning God's Son, "who was descended from David according to the flesh and was declared to be the Son of God in power . . . by his resurrection from the dead" (ROMANS 1:3-4). So in his human nature Jesus is the son of David, but in his divine nature he is David's Lord. And the Resurrection is the supreme public revelation of his true identity.

The earliest Christian confession of faith was this simple, three-word declaration: "Jesus is Lord!" (cf. 1 CORINTHIANS 12:3). This is the conviction that turned the world upside down in the first century A.D., and that continues to do so in the 21st century, wherever and whenever it is seriously lived out. In A.D. 112 a Roman governor named Pliny wrote the emperor Trajan for instructions on how to deal with the sect of the Christians that was growing rapidly in his province. Thinking he ought to provide the emperor with a bit of background, Pliny did some research into the practices of the Christians (he reports that he obtained his information by torturing a couple of Christian slave girls). In passing on what he learned to Trajan, Pliny provides us with the earliest description of Christian worship written by a non-Christian. It begins this way: "One day a week the Christians gather early in the morning, before dawn, and sing a hymn to Christ as to a god."

Christians have always worshiped Jesus as God. That, at a bare minimum, is what defines us. When we stand with Christians of all times and places and confess that Jesus is Lord, we are saying many things about who he is and what is due to him. But first and foremost we are saying that he is God.

The depictions of Christ we usually see tend to emphasize either his gentleness and compassion, as revealed in the days of his earthly ministry, or his agonized suffering on the cross. Jesus the Good Shepherd, Christ the Light of the World, the Praying Savior in Gethsemane, the Head Crowned with Thorns—these are the images that hang on our walls, illustrate our Bibles, and, nowadays, adorn our T-shirts. They all may be appropriate, but they need to be balanced by a picture of the risen Christ as he looks now, or at least as he appeared to John on Patmos.

> Then I turned to see the voice that was speaking to me, and . . . I saw . . . one like a son of man, clothed with a long robe and with a golden sash around his chest. The hairs of his head were white like wool, as white as snow. His eyes were like a flame of fire, his feet were like burnished bronze, refined in a furnace, and his voice was like the roar of many waters. In his right hand he held seven stars, from his mouth came a sharp two-edged sword, and his face was like the sun shining in full strength.
>
> When I saw him, I fell at his feet as though dead.
>
> —*Revelation 1:12-17a*

Jesus Is Reigning

So the first great affirmation of Psalm 110:1 relates to Jesus' identity as Lord. A second thing this verse does is tell us what Christ the Lord is presently doing. It proclaims that he is enthroned now at the Father's right hand. In other words, Jesus is reigning in sovereign authority over the universe. The writer to the Hebrews quotes Psalm 110:1 to assert Christ's superiority to every other being in existence, including the highest and mightiest angelic powers. Hebrews 1 consists largely of Old Testament quotations, mostly from the Psalms, strung together to assert the supremacy of Christ. At the conclusion of the chapter the writer asks, "to which of the angels has [God] ever said, 'Sit at my right hand until I make your enemies a footstool for your feet'?" (HEBREWS 1:13). The apostle makes a similar point in the opening chapter of Ephesians, where he says that God raised Christ from the dead

> and seated him at his right hand in the heavenly places, far above all rule and authority and power and dominion, and above every name that is named, not only in this age but also in the one to come.
>
> —*Ephesians 1:20-21*

He is not only above all other powers and principalities; he is *far* above them. He is not only far above all other powers in *this* age, but also in the age to come. Jesus is first; anything or anyone else, in this world or any other world there might be, is a distant second.

When the New Testament writers talk about Christ seated at God's right hand, they never meant this to be taken literally, as if God the Father and Christ the Son are both lounging on golden chairs somewhere above the clouds. If you stop and think about it, of course you will realize that God has neither a right hand nor a literal throne. We use the same kind of figurative language today. For example, when a news reporter says, "The White House announced today that it was doing such and such," he doesn't mean that a building in Washington D.C. started talking to the press. That famous place serves as a symbol of the administration's authority. In the same way, for Jesus to be lifted up from earth to heaven and exalted to God's right hand simply means that God has given him the place of highest honor and greatest authority.

The Father has made the Son his Executive Officer. "Why [does the creed add] the next words, 'and is seated at the right hand of God'?" asks the Heidelberg Catechism. And it answers, "Christ ascended to heaven, there to show that he is head of his church, and that the Father rules all things through him" (Q. & A. 50). Christ is reigning. Byzantine churches are always decorated with a profusion of icons and frescoes. The walls and ceilings feature images of bishops and angels, prophets and apostles; scenes from the Bible and the lives of the saints. But the same figure is always depicted on the church's central dome, that spreads like the vault of heaven over the heads of the worshipers. It is Christ the Lord, seated on his throne in glory. And the title above his head is *ho Pantokrator:* The Ruler of All.

Jesus Is Waiting

There is a third truth about Jesus proclaimed by Psalm 110:1. We're told his identity: Jesus is Lord. We are given a picture suggesting his activity: he reigns with supreme authority over all things. But we are also reminded that God's redemptive work is not yet complete. "Sit at my right hand, *until* I make your enemies your footstool." Christ the Lord is reigning, but he is also waiting. "When Christ had offered for all time a single sacrifice for sins, he sat down at the right hand of God, waiting from that time until his enemies should be made a footstool for his feet" (Hebrews 10:12-13, in yet another citation of Psalm 110:1). Christ the Lord is seated in majesty and power at the right hand of the Father. His saving work is accomplished. His pain and shame are over and done with. He is no longer the humiliated sufferer. Now the crucified One has become the exalted One, as the book of Revelation makes clear. To Christ the Lord belong all blessing and honor and glory and power.

These things are already his in heaven. But Christ does not yet receive the honor and praise of all on earth. The Lord's enemies continue to rage against him, and against his people as well. They haven't yet been put under his feet. And so, he waits. And evil, and pain, and injustice, and innocent suffering go on and on, prompting us to cry out with the saints of old, "O Lord, How long?" (PSALM 94:3, REVELATION 6:10).

We don't know the answer. We don't know how long it will be until the Father keeps his promise to the Son and makes all his enemies his footstool. So we wait, too. But we do know that day will come.

One of the greatest of all New Testament passages bearing witness to the ultimate triumph of the Lord Jesus is the Christ hymn of Philippians 2:6-11, written in praise of Christ Jesus,

> who, though he was in the form of God, did not count equality with God a thing to be grasped, but made himself nothing, taking the form of a servant, being born in the likeness of men. And being found in human form, he humbled himself by becoming obedient to the point of death, even death on a cross. Therefore God has highly exalted him and bestowed on him the name that is above every name, so that at the name of Jesus every knee should bow, in heaven and on earth and under the earth, and every tongue confess that Jesus Christ is Lord, to the glory of God the Father.

The hymn follows Christ's descent from the glories of the Godhead along the hard path of humility and obedience into the shame and suffering of the lowest kind of death, death on a cross. But God has responded to Jesus' obedience by exalting him to the highest place of all and bestowing on him "the name that is above every name." And so, the hymn concludes, one day every knee will bow in heaven and on earth and under the earth, and every tongue will confess that Jesus Christ is Lord, to the glory of God the Father. The truth will be seen and known and acknowledged by all. Jesus' claims will be openly vindicated before the whole creation and Jesus Christ the Lord will receive the honor that is his due. There will be no dissenting voices. On that day all his enemies will either be turned into his friends or put under his feet.

MEANWHILE . . .

Meanwhile, we continue to confess with the church through the ages, *Kurios Iesous,* "Jesus is Lord!" (1 CORINTHIANS 12:3). This is not merely religious cheerleading. To say "Christ is Lord" is to say considerably more than "I ♡ Jesus." It is also more than just an expression of our own personal faith. It is a cosmic claim about the way things really are. N. T. Wright, the Anglican Bishop of Durham and a leading New Testament theologian, explains something of the significance of this confession of our faith.

> The claim that "Jesus is Lord" was never, in the first century, what we would call a religious claim pure and simple. There was no such thing as religion pure and simple. It was a claim about an ultimate reality which included politics, culture, commerce, family life, and everything else you could think of. And if you stop saying "Jesus is Lord" out of deference to the private opinions of your friends and neighbors, Caesar smiles his grim smile and extends his empire by one more street.[18]

Today more than ever we need to have the courage of our convictions. If we want to be Christians in the New Testament sense of the word, we must confess before the world that Christ is Lord in every sphere of life. But if Christ is Lord, he is Lord of everything and everyone. He may not be, of course. It's possible the apostles were wrong about him. "If Christ has not been raised . . . we are of all people most to be pitied," as Paul saw clearly (1 CORINTHIANS 15:17, 19). But what is not possible is that the biblical witness to Christ as Lord is true, but that it also doesn't really matter to everyone. What is not possible is what so many Christians today seem to be saying: "Jesus is my Lord, but you are free to choose someone else as your Lord. I wouldn't want to impose my beliefs on you." That just won't cut it. If Jesus is not *the* Lord, he can't be anyone's Lord. And if he *is* Lord, then he's also the only Lord there is. Put it this way. If you celebrate Easter, you'd better be celebrating world evangelization, too.

But in addition to proclaiming the universal lordship of Jesus Christ, we need to be advancing it as well, one street at a time. The fact that we must wait until the Father makes Christ's rule public and triumphant does not mean that meanwhile we do nothing but talk and sing. Our waiting (and his) isn't passive or quiescent; it's the waiting of faith, not inactivity. And so we live our lives as if Jesus *is* Lord of all—not just of our homes and families and churches, but of our businesses and schools and communities and countries.

The biblical vision of Christ the Lord, enthroned at God's right hand, waiting until his enemies are subdued, can help us maintain a healthy spiritual balance. We will not fall for the naive optimism of secular utopians who think that human perfectability is just around the next technological corner, or that with a bit more education and effort and good will we can establish heaven on earth. But neither will we give in to the cynicism and bleak despair of those who recognize that the perfect society never comes. We will not adopt the escapist mentality of some Christians who think the only thing to do is to try to pluck some "brands from the burning" while you wait to be raptured. But neither will we clam up about the claims of Christ and the need for people to recognize him as Lord, and bow the knee to him.

So let's do this. Let's live in such a way as will bear witness to the lordship of Christ. Let's begin to incarnate the values of the kingdom of God, the shalom of universal righteousness and flourishing, starting in our own homes and churches and communities. That means seeking justice for all, especially the disadvantaged and dispossessed. The biblical vision of Christ's lordship prompts us to fight pollution, and corruption, and disease, and poverty, and racism, and a host of other social and environmental ills. It calls Christians to practice all the arts that make for human well-being and enrichment. We create beauty, we speak truth, we love people, we serve and honor God. And we share Jesus with everyone in the world—all as we wait for the Father's promise.

What Are You Living For?

The vision of Christ the Lord, enthroned at God's right hand, fires my imagination. It also prompts reflection on a basic question—what is the real purpose of my life. The early church Father Tertullian was pointing out the radical difference between the pagan values of classical Greece and the worldview of the Bible when he asked his famous question, "What has Athens to do with Jerusalem?" At no point were those two belief systems in greater conflict than in their understanding of what people should live for. The *Iliad* describes how Achilles, greatest of all the Greek heroes fighting against Troy, was given a momentous choice when he was told what Fate had decreed for him. He could go home and enjoy a long and happy life, or stay at Troy and win glory. But he would also perish in the war. Achilles chose glory in a heartbeat, because to a Greek, personal glory meant everything—even if it cost him his life. You might recall a very different decision made by the young King Solomon. When offered his choice of anything God had it in his power to give, he asked for wisdom; which, as Solomon himself would later teach us, begins with the fear of the Lord.

So what are you living for? Pagans still live for personal glory, in one form or another. But for Christians the only glory that matters is the Lord's. "God forbid that I should glory, save in the cross of our

Lord Jesus Christ" (GALATIANS 6:14, KJV). The only fame we care about is the fame of Jesus' name. Christians live for the Lord. "If we live, we live to the Lord . . ." (ROMANS 14:8). And Christians live for the kingdom. "Seek first the kingdom of God and his righteousness . . ." (MATTHEW 6:33). We know we will not create the kingdom of God by our efforts. The kingdom will come only by the power of the Son at the pleasure of the Father. But until that happens, we will go on living for the Lord and his kingdom rather than for wealth or fame or power or pleasure.

Because Christ *is* the Lord.

Study Questions

1. Why were the New Testament writers so interested in Psalm 110:1? List three truths about Jesus the New Testament writers drew out of Psalm 110:1.

2. What does the confession "Jesus is Lord" really mean for life outside of church? What difficulties do Christians encounter in making this confession in their everyday lives?

3. Explain how Christ's resurrection from the dead authenticates the riddle Jesus put to the Pharisees in Matthew 22:41-46. Be sure to consider Romans 1:3-4.

4. What does Scripture mean when it says that Christ is seated at the right hand of the Father in heaven? Does this biblical imagery have political implications? How does this connect with the confession of Christ's lordship?

5. David Bast writes: "To say 'Christ is Lord' is to say something considerably more than 'I ♡ Jesus.' It is also more than just an expression of our own personal faith. It is a cosmic claim about the way things really are." Explain what this means in your own words.

6. True or False: Since only Christians believe Jesus is Lord, the good they might do in the world is intended to benefit just them and their friends. If you think this statement is false, how would you reword it to make it true?

Chapter 6

Christ Our High Priest

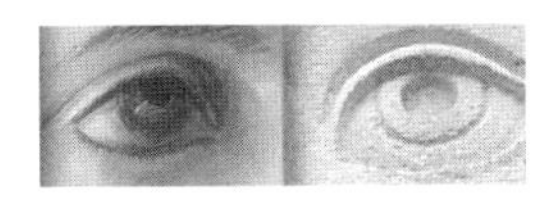

PSALM 110:4
HEBREWS 5:1-11

The LORD has sworn
and will not change his mind,
"You are a priest forever
after the order of Melchizedek."

—*Psalm 110:4*

For every high priest chosen from among men is appointed to act on behalf of men in relation to God, to offer gifts and sacrifices for sins. He can deal gently with the ignorant and wayward, since he himself is beset with weakness. Because of this he is obligated to offer sacrifice for his own sins just as he does for those of the people. And no one takes this honor for himself, but only when called by God, just as Aaron was.

So also Christ did not exalt himself to be made a high priest, but was appointed by him who said to him,

> "You are my Son,
> today I have begotten you";
>
> as he says also in another place,
>
> "You are a priest forever,
> after the order of Melchizedek."
>
> In the days of his flesh, Jesus offered up prayers and supplications, with loud cries and tears, to him who was able to save him from death, and he was heard because of his reverence. Although he was a son, he learned obedience through what he suffered. And being made perfect, he became the source of eternal salvation to all who obey him, being designated by God a high priest after the order of Melchizedek.
>
> About this we have much to say, and it is hard to explain . . .
>
> —*Hebrews 5:1-11a*

An Essay by C. S. Lewis entitled "The Psalms" begins this way.

> The dominant impression I get from reading the Psalms is one of antiquity. I seem to be looking into a deep pit of time, but looking through a lens which brings the figures who inhabit that depth up close to my eye. In that momentary proximity they are almost shockingly alien; creatures of unrestrained emotion, wallowing in self-pity, sobbing, cursing, screaming in exultation, clashing uncouth weapons or dancing to the din of strange musical instruments.[19]

It's not just the Psalms; the whole Bible is an alien book in many ways. For those of us who are familiar with it some of the strangeness may have worn off, but all you have to do is look more closely to see it. For instance, how involved are you with the ritual slaughter of animals?

How recently have you worried about becoming ceremonially unclean? But concepts like these lie behind not just the Old Testament but the argument of New Testament books like Hebrews as well.

Hebrews was written to encourage believers who had left Judaism to become followers of Jesus, but who were now feeling considerable pressure to return to the old faith. That pressure came in several forms. There were, of course, ties of family and tradition pulling them back. There was also increasing persecution against Christians throughout the Roman world. Perhaps most significantly, Jewish teachers were arguing that Christianity was inferior to its Old Testament predecessor. The relationship between church and synagogue was growing strained, a fact anticipated in New Testament texts such as Matthew 10:16-23. Furthermore, Jewish apologists were comparing Jesus unfavorably with Moses, the great lawgiver, and his brother Aaron, the high priest. In fact, while Judaism could still boast of a priesthood descended from Aaron, the Christian religion didn't even have priests. Its leaders were pastors and teachers. It offered no atoning sacrifices for sin. So how could it possibly be as good as Judaism? So, we may surmise, the arguments went.

The Order of Melchizedek

Hebrews' response follows what seems like a rather strange line to us, and it begins in a very unusual place. The writer turns once more to Psalm 110. The psalm opens with a prophecy about a victorious divine Lord who is enthroned by God at his right hand.

> The LORD says to my Lord:
> "Sit at my right hand,
> until I make your enemies your footstool." (V. 1)

That's a verse to which Hebrews draws repeated attention, as we have seen. But later in the psalm comes a further divine decree. God declares that the Lord whom he exalts will also be a priest.

> The LORD has sworn

and will not change his mind,
"You are a priest forever
after the order of Melchizedek." (V. 4)

The writer of Hebrews seized upon that verse—Psalm 110:4—and made it the linchpin of his argument. Just as the first verse of Psalm 110 reveals the divine lordship of Jesus, so verse four testifies to his priestly office. Six of Hebrews' thirteen chapters (chapters 5–10) deal with the subject of Jesus our Great High Priest, who is superior in every way to all who had gone before. In these chapters the writer carefully lists Christ's qualifications for the priesthood. Anyone, including Jesus, had to meet certain requirements in order to be a proper priest. First, he had to represent his people, that is, he had to be one of them (HEBREWS 5:1). The priest had to be "chosen from among men," as Hebrews says; he had to be truly human. And so the writer delights in emphasizing the full, real humanity of Jesus Christ.

> In the days of his flesh, Jesus offered up prayers and supplications, with loud cries and tears, to him who was able to save him from death, and he was heard because of his reverence. Although he was a son, he learned obedience through what he suffered.
>
> —*Hebrews 5:7-8*

Second, a priest had to be called and ordained by God for his office. "And no one takes this honor for himself, but only when called by God, just as Aaron was" (HEBREWS 5:4). No legitimate priest could be self-appointed. Gaining the high-priesthood wasn't like being elected president. You couldn't run for the office and win it through clever campaigning or lavish spending. In the Old Testament only the descendants of Aaron, of the tribe of Levi, qualified for the priestly office. But Jesus was not a Levite; he was from the tribe of Judah, descended from the house of David. So how could he be a priest at all, let alone the ultimate High Priest? The answer is that God chose and appointed him directly, as foretold in the Psalms.

So also Christ did not exalt himself to be made a high priest, but was appointed by him who said to him,

> "You are my Son,
> today I have begotten you";

as he also says in another place,

> "You are a priest forever,
> after the order of Melchizedek."
>
> —*Hebrews 5:5-6*

The writer to the Hebrews finds biblical precedent for the concept of an unusual priesthood. It was Psalm 110:4 that suggested this, based on the psalmist's reading of an even earlier episode from Old Testament history. And so the writer of Hebrews, following the psalmist, takes us back to one of the truly puzzling stories in the Bible. This strange incident, from the early chapters of the book of Genesis, provided both a precedent and a model for Jesus' unique priesthood. That model was the mysterious Melchizedek, whom Genesis describes as "king of Salem [that is, Jerusalem]," and a "priest of God Most High" (GENESIS 14:18). When we read that we think: who in the world was Melchizedek, and how did he get to be a priest of the one true God while ruling as the king of Jerusalem? Where did he come from? How did he come to know the Lord? What became of him later?

But to all these questions the Bible gives no answers at all. The writer to the Hebrews, who spills way more ink over Melchizedek than any other biblical author, only heightens the mystery by what he says. Hebrews sees in Melchizedek a foreshadowing of Christ. Because Abraham offered his tithe to Melchizedek and was blessed by him, it's clear that Melchizedek is superior even to Abraham. And, as a matter of course (to the biblical way of thinking anyway), superior to all Abraham's descendants as well (see HEBREWS 7:1-2, 4-10). Moreover, because Melchizedek has no beginning or end (at least in terms of the biblical narrative he doesn't, which is all that Hebrews is concerned with) he is an "eternal" priest, just like Jesus (7:3, 23-25).

As our writer dryly remarks, all this business about "a high priest after the order of Melchizedek" (5:10) "is hard to explain" (5:11). But his main point is clear. Christ is fully qualified to be a priest. In fact, he is far superior to all human priests because of his sinless perfection. Every high priest had to offer sacrifices for himself first of all. So how could such a man possibly offer a perfect once-for-all sacrifice for others? But Jesus is different: "Unlike the other high priests," says Hebrews, "he does not need to offer sacrifices day after day, first for his own sins, and then for the sins of the people. He sacrificed for their sins once for all when he offered himself" (7:27 NIV).

Our Intercessor

Earlier in this book (chapter 2) we focused on the sacrifice that Jesus as High Priest offered once for all for the sins of the world—the sacrifice of his own body. Because Jesus died for sin on the cross, all who belong to him are forgiven, fully and forever. No other sacrifice is needed; none other is even possible. All we need do is trust in him, and salvation is ours.

But it is also important to reflect on what it means to have Christ living right now as our priest. Once again Hebrews instructs us:

> For it is witnessed of him,
>
> > "You are a priest forever,
> > after the order of Melchizedek."
>
> On the one hand, a former commandment is set aside because of its weakness and uselessness (for the law made nothing perfect); but on the other hand, a better hope is introduced, through which we draw near to God.
>
> And it was not without an oath. For those who formerly became priests were made such without an oath, but this one was made a priest with an oath by the one who said to him:

> "The Lord has sworn
> and will not change his mind,
> 'You are a priest forever.'"
>
> This makes Jesus the guarantor of a better covenant.
>
> The former priests were many in number, because they were prevented by death from continuing in office, but he holds his priesthood permanently, because he continues forever. Consequently, he is able to save to the uttermost those who draw near to God through him, since he always lives to make intercession for them.
>
> —*Hebrews 7:17-25*

Because Christ is alive forevermore, says our writer, "he is able to save to the uttermost those who draw near to God through him, since he always lives to make intercession for them." That echoes what Paul wrote to the Romans: "Christ Jesus is the one who died—more than that, who was raised—who is at the right hand of God, who indeed is interceding for us" (ROMANS 8:34). So, concludes Hebrews, ". . . we *have* a great priest over the house of God" (10:21). We have a great priest, present tense. Jesus did pay for our sins, once for all. That's finished. But his priestly work for us (as our Mediator) is far from over. The apostle John writes,

> My little children, I am writing these things to you so that you may not sin. But if anyone does sin, we have an advocate with the Father, Jesus Christ the righteous.
>
> —*1 John 2:1*

Moreover, as a divine high priest who is also truly human, Jesus can sympathize with our weaknesses (HEBREWS 4:15). He really has identified with us. He has felt every temptation and sorrow or pain that we might experience. He knows firsthand whatever it is we're going through. And he will help us get through it, no matter what the trouble.

In fact, right now Christ is praying for us. I think about what that means and try to imagine how it works. What does Christ ask for when he intercedes with the Father for me? Perhaps he prays for God to do the same thing in my life as he did in Jesus' life: "Father, glorify your name" (JOHN 12:28). Perhaps he prays as he once prayed for his disciples: "Holy Father, keep them in your name" (JOHN 17:11). Not only does Jesus pray for me, the Holy Spirit does as well (see ROMANS 8:26-27). What affect does it have on me to be continually taken up and remembered and blessed in the inner conversation of the Trinity? I can't begin to fathom that. But I am sure of this: these prayers on my behalf will be answered. And it will take an eternity for me to experience what all the answers will mean.

Hold Fast and Draw Near

So what should we do in response to this truth? Hebrews tells us in plain and simple terms. Because Christ is such a high priest, we need to *hold fast* and *draw near.*

First of all then, hold fast. We must "hold firmly to the faith we profess," says the writer (4:14, NIV cf. 10:23). There can be no going back for Christians, not to an old religion, or to former practices, or to a different way of life. If you know Christ there's no one and nothing better to go back to. Just hold on to the fact that right now Jesus Christ—who is seated at the right hand of God the Father, far above all powers and authorities (EPHESIANS 1:20-21)—is praying for you. What more could you ask for?

So there's nothing better than Jesus to go back to. And there's nothing more than Jesus to add to him. You don't need any other go-between. You don't need a human priest to put you right with God. You don't need saints or angels to intercede for you. You don't need to perform some ritual or ceremony or make sacrifices to get God on your side. You don't need to add a rabbit's foot to Jesus' prayers, for luck. You've got Jesus; stick to him, and him alone! Believing in Christ as our priestly intercessor delivers us from every kind of religious fear or superstition, and gives us the same confident assurance that the apostle Paul enjoyed.

> If God is for us, who can be against us? He who did not spare his own Son but gave him up for us all, how will he not also with him graciously give us all things? . . . Who shall bring any charge against God's elect? It is God who justifies. Who is to condemn? Christ Jesus is the one who died—more than that, who was raised—who is at the right hand of God, who indeed is interceding for us. Who shall separate us from the love of Christ? Shall tribulation, or distress, or persecution, or famine, or nakedness, or danger, or sword? . . . No, in all these things we are more than conquerors through him who loved us. For I am sure that neither death nor life, nor angels nor rulers, nor things present nor things to come, nor powers, nor height nor depth, nor anything else in all creation, will be able to separate us from the love of God in Christ Jesus our Lord.
>
> —*Romans 8:31-39*

The other lesson Hebrews takes from Jesus our Great High Priest is that we must draw near to God through him.

> . . . and since we have a great priest over the house of God, let us draw near . . . . (10:21-22)

Because of this great and compassionate priest we have a tremendous privilege: free and open access to God himself. We can come with boldness even, assured of a welcome. Entering the throne room of an ancient ruler was a frightening (and potentially deadly) experience—just think of Queen Esther (see ESTHER 4:10–5:2). But because Jesus is our high priest we need never fear or hesitate to come into the presence of the highest and holiest Sovereign of all—the eternal and almighty God of the universe. A famous picture published many years ago in *LIFE* magazine showed President John F. Kennedy standing behind his desk in the Oval Office, his arms folded, talking to an aide. But underneath the desk Kennedy's little boy, John-John, was playing at the president's feet. The difference Jesus' priestly ministry makes for us is the difference between the aide in that picture and the son. Because of Christ we can always be sure of our welcome, confident in our Father's presence.

This is what we find when we draw near to God through Christ: not anger and punishment, but mercy and grace and help in our need (cf. HEBREWS 4:16). So "Come to the Father through Jesus the Son," as Fanny Crosby taught us to sing. The way is open! Hebrews isn't just talking about salvation here. It's talking about our ordinary worship, and especially our prayer life. Since we have daily need for mercy, so we should approach God every day through Christ. In the Old Testament you may remember that only the high priest could enter the Holy of Holies, and he just once a year on the Day of Atonement. But now all who trust in Jesus' blood and righteousness may come. The way is open in him—to anyone, at any time. Just as the curtain separating the Holy Place in the temple from the Holy of Holies was miraculously torn in two when Jesus died, so the way to God now is open because Jesus' body was torn on the cross. Hebrews calls this "a new and living way" because it's based on the death and resurrection of Jesus. Access to God through Christ is for everyone who will come, not just for the special few or those who deserve to be there.

Of course, the Christians to whom the book of Hebrews was originally addressed had a real advantage over us. They came at the end of a thousand years of temple worship, a thousand *Yom Kippurs* with the high priest walking tremblingly into the Holy of Holies to apply the sacrificial blood to the mercy seat. The unmistakable message of all those years and all those ceremonies would have been engrained in them: access to the Holy One is restricted. How excited they must have been to hear that Jesus now had opened a new way for every believer. What joy it must have given them to freely approach God and call him "Abba" in Jesus' name. We come from the opposite direction: 2,000 years of Christian privilege. More than that, ours is an age that has very little sense any longer that "our God is a consuming fire" (HEBREWS 12:29). So our prayers tend to be casual, complacent, perfunctory, flippant, presumptuous. Perhaps if we had more of the Old Testament's sense of the awful majesty of God we would feel more wonder and gratitude at the New Testament's witness to Christ our high priest, and the free access to God we have through him.

Before the throne of God above
I have a strong and perfect plea.
A great high Priest whose Name is Love
Who ever lives and pleads for me.
My name is graven on His hands,
My name is written on His heart.
I know that while in heaven He stands
No tongue can bid me thence depart.

When Satan tempts me to despair
And tells me of the guilt within,
Upward I look and see Him there
Who made an end of all my sin.
Because the sinless Savior died
My sinful soul is counted free.
For God the just is satisfied
To look on Him and pardon me.

Behold Him there the risen Lamb,
My perfect spotless righteousness,
The great unchangeable I AM,
The King of glory and of grace,
One in Himself I cannot die.
My soul is purchased by His blood,
My life is hid with Christ on high,
With Christ my Savior and my God!

—Charitie Bancroft (1841-1923)

Study Questions

1. What characteristics of Jesus' priestly office can be drawn from Psalm 110:4 and Hebrews 5:1-10? List three items that point to Jesus' priestly qualifications.

2. How are Jesus and Melchizedek similar as priests? How are they different? Why do the similarities and differences matter?

3. Most Christians have a good grasp that Christ's substitutionary death paid for our sin debt, once for all, but Christ's work as Mediator on our behalf is present tense. Christ's active, ongoing priestly role is why Protestant churches reject the use of human priestly mediators. Yet, most recognize that there is some value in being publicly accountable for our sin. What, if anything, can be done to increase accountability for sin in Protestant churches?

4. Why do you think that more believers don't "draw near" to God (HEBREWS 10:21-22), especially since Christ has provided open access to the very throne room of heaven?

5. What can Christians do, without reverting to some form of legalism, to recapture a sense of the awful majesty of God? Why is it so much harder to live a God-honoring life out of gratitude than out of fear?

Chapter 7

Christ Our King

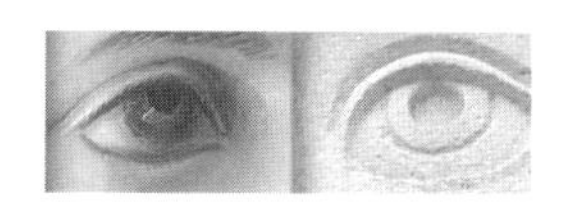

PSALM 45:1-9
HEBREWS 1:7-9

My heart overflows with a pleasing theme;
I address my verses to the king;
    my tongue is like the pen of a ready scribe.

You are the most handsome of the sons of men;
    grace is poured upon your lips;
    therefore God has blessed you forever.
Gird your sword on your thigh, O mighty one,
    in your splendor and majesty!

In your majesty ride out victoriously
    for the cause of truth and meekness and righteousness;
    let your right hand teach you awesome deeds!
Your arrows are sharp
    in the heart of the king's enemies;
    the peoples fall under you.

Your throne, O God, is forever and ever.
    The scepter of your kingdom is a scepter of uprightness;

you have loved righteousness and hated wickedness.
Therefore God, your God, has anointed you
with the oil of gladness beyond your companions;

your robes are all fragrant with myrrh and aloes and cassia.
From ivory palaces stringed instruments make you glad;
daughters of kings are among your ladies of honor;
at your right hand stands the queen in gold of Ophir.

—Psalm 45:1-9

Of the angels [God] says,
'He makes his angels winds, and his ministers a flame of fire.'
But of the Son he says,
'Your throne, O God, is forever and ever,
the scepter of uprightness is the scepter of your kingdom.'
You have loved righteousness and hated wickedness;
therefore God, your God, has anointed you with the oil of gladness beyond your companions.

—Hebrews 1:7-9

Charles Hodge taught biblical and systematic theology at Princeton Seminary from 1822 until his death in 1878. He was then succeeded by his son, Archibald Alexander (or A.A., as he is usually known.) The Hodges, father and son, were the outstanding theologians of 19th-century America, together serving as the leading lights of what came to be called "Old School" Presbyterianism, or Reformed orthodoxy.

On June 23, 1833, when A. A. Hodge was still a ten-year-old living with his family in Princeton, he gave a letter that he had co-written with his sister Mary Elizabeth to a seminary graduate who was about to depart for missionary service in Ceylon. The Hodge children addressed their letter to the "heathen," using that term in its 19th-century sense as referring simply to non-Christians.

Dear Heathen:
The Lord Jesus Christ hath promised that the time shall come

> when all the ends of the earth shall be His kingdom. And God is not a man that He should lie nor the son of man that He should repent. And if this was promised by a Being who cannot lie, why do you not help it to come sooner by reading the Bible, and attending to the words of your teachers, and loving God, and, renouncing your idols, take Christianity into your temples? And soon there will not be a Nation, no, not a space of ground as large as a footstep, that will [need] a missionary. My sister and myself have, by small self-denials, procured two dollars which are enclosed in this letter to buy tracts and Bibles to teach you.
>
> —*Archibald Alexander Hodge, and Mary Elizabeth Hodge, Friends of the Heathen*[20]

You might be impressed by this letter's style (not bad for a couple of children) or touched by the example of their sacrificial support of missions ($2 was a lot of money to earn in 1833 by "small self-denials"). You might also be charmed by their naive, childish appeal to the Hindus and Buddhists of Sri Lanka that they simply believe the missionaries who teach them the Bible and take Christianity into their temples (what could be simpler?). But what I find most compelling is the command of biblical theology displayed by these children. Christ is King! they affirm, and there's not one place on earth where that isn't so, or that will not someday know it. As Abraham Kuyper would declare two generations later, there isn't an inch of ground anywhere in the world of which Christ does not claim, "This is mine!" Nor, insists young A. A. Hodge, is there one person anywhere who does not need to hear and acknowledge this truth right now.

In Praise of the King

In Psalm 45, the writer sings the praises of Israel's king on his wedding day. This psalm proclaims the king's beauty and grace, his strength, his splendor, his righteousness.

> My heart overflows with a pleasing theme;

I address my verses to the king;
my tongue is like the pen of a ready scribe.

You are the most handsome of the sons of men;
grace is poured upon your lips;
therefore God has blessed you forever.
Gird your sword on your thigh, O mighty one,
in your splendor and majesty!

In your majesty ride out victoriously
for the cause of truth and meekness and righteousness;
let your right hand teach you awesome deeds!

—*Psalm 45:1-4*

What a picture! The book of Psalms features a number of poems like this, written originally to glorify the rulers of the house of David. These royal psalms usually celebrate a special occasion—a coronation, such as in Psalm 2, or a marriage, as here in Psalm 45. But their full significance isn't found in the circumstances of their original composition. Scholars tell us that the final collection and editing of the book of Psalms took place in the post-exilic period. This is to say, the book we now know as the Psalms came into being only *after* the survivors of the Babylonian captivity returned from exile to live in Jerusalem again.

But think about their situation then. The city of Jerusalem lay in ruins. It would be a hundred years before Nehemiah would return to restore its walls. When the temple was rebuilt, the old-timers who could still remember Solomon's glorious building wept at the contrast (EZRA 3:12). In the aftermath of the physical destruction of their country and spiritual devastation of exile, the Jewish people struggled to make a living amidst the wreckage of their lives. They labored apprehensively to re-fortify Jerusalem in the face of the taunts and threats of their enemies, who surrounded them. Judea was no longer an independent country, but merely a province of the mighty Persian Empire. Most significantly, there was no longer a king in Jerusalem; there never would be again, never another son of David reigning over the City of David. So the question is, why include in the Psalter all these royal songs praising the house of David, and celebrating occasions that would never come again? Is it all just nostalgia? Are these royal psalms one big exercise in escapism or fantasy?

The Once and Future King

The answer is No. The royal psalms don't just look backward; they point forward, to the true King of Israel. In 1958 T. H. White published a novel about King Arthur entitled *The Once and Future King.* That title could well be written over each of the royal psalms in the Psalter, and over Psalm 45 especially. No Old Testament believer doubted that one day the real King would come. David would return in the person of his son, the Messiah. He would be the ideal, of whom all the old kings—and all human rulers of whatever kind—were, at best, only approximations. This King would reign forever in perfect justice and matchless splendor, with his beautiful consort at his side (see verses 10-17 of PSALM 45). So as they remembered and sang and prayed the songs that celebrated the king, these Hebrew faithful looked not backward but forward, to the day of their King's appearing.

When Jesus came into the world, it didn't take his disciples long to figure out the true identity of the One to whom these royal psalms pointed. The first chapter of Hebrews is devoted to a comparison between Jesus and the angels. Now that may seem like an odd choice of subject to us, but it was a hot topic in the first century. As the worship of Jesus spread further and further, people—especially Jewish people—tried to come to grips with just who this awesome figure really was. Maybe he's an angel, some suggested, perhaps even a sort of super-angel. The writer to the Hebrews dismisses this suggestion by contrasting what God says about angels and what he says about the Son. Quoting from the Psalms, the writer of Hebrews observes,

> Of the angels [God] says,
>
> > " 'He makes his angels winds,
> > and his ministers a flame of fire."

But of the Son he says,

> "'Your throne, O God, is forever and ever,
> the scepter of uprightness is the scepter of your kingdom.'
> You have loved righteousness and hated wickedness;
> therefore God, your God, has anointed you with the oil of gladness beyond your companions.'"
>
> —*Hebrews 1:7-9, quoting Psalm 104:4 and Psalm 45:6-7*

So the eternal king, whose throne is forever and ever, is King Jesus. In fact, he is not just king, he is God. "Your throne, O *God,* is forever and ever." This is the bedrock conviction on which the whole New Testament is based. The first Christians proclaimed the message that Jesus of Nazareth, the man they had known and followed for three years throughout Galilee and Judea, the prophet and teacher who had been crucified by the Romans, was in fact the King of the universe, and was presently seated on the throne of God. Can we really wrap our minds around how amazing that claim is? Where in the world did a group of first-century Jews come up with this idea? The answer is simple. What made them first believe and then publicize this audacious claim was the conviction that Jesus had literally been raised from the dead and exalted to divine glory.

Since Christ Is on the Throne

Let's think about what it means for us that Christ is our King. In an earlier chapter we focused on Christ the Lord. His lordship and kingship are obviously closely related ideas. In chapter 5 we considered the implications of the truth that Christ is Lord for our lives, in particular, for our actions. As Christians we must proclaim the message that Jesus is Lord, to everyone everywhere, and witness to the reality of his lordship by living out the values of the kingdom. Here let's think about what "Christ the King" means for our beliefs, our faith, and our assurance.

The fact that Christ is King means first of all that his church is eternally secure. All who belong to him belong to him forever. I remember in seminary reading a comment of Calvin's that because Christ is an eternal king, he will never lack for subjects. I have never forgotten that. We say that it takes followers to make a leader; Christ is a leader who creates his own followers, and then preserves and protects them forever. Sometimes when we look at the state of the church we could be tempted to despair, or at least to be really, really discouraged—so much worldliness and sin, so much superficiality, so little real faith, such poor and fumbling obedience. But then I think, wait a minute! Those characteristics don't just apply to the church "out there," as if it were some abstract thing. They describe me! When we are feeling oppressed by the rising tide of secularism in our culture, or disheartened at the pathetic state of so much that passes for "church life," or especially when we are discouraged by our own personal failures as followers of Jesus, we must not lose hope.

Remember this: the King will reign forever and ever. And he also has a queen—

> Hear, O daughter, and consider,
> and incline your ear:
> forget your people and your father's house,
> and the king will desire your beauty.
> Since he is your lord, bow to him.
>
> —*Psalm 45:10-11*

The church is the bride of Christ, which means this for those of us who are members of it: Christ is not only our King, he is our husband. "For your Maker is your husband, the LORD of hosts is his name; and the Holy One of Israel is your Redeemer" (ISAIAH 54:5). Jesus is the Lover of our souls. When we stumble or fall, when we are overwhelmed by a sense of our sins and shortcomings, he comes to us with the same question he asked Peter, again and again: "Do you love me?" And if we can say, with Peter, "Lord, you know I love you," then all will be well. Despite all our blemishes, we are beautiful in our King's eyes, and his promise to us is that he will one day present us spotless before the throne. Then we shall reign with him.

In place of your fathers shall be your sons;
you will make them princes in all the earth.
I will cause your name to be remembered in all generations;
therefore nations will praise you forever and ever.

—Psalm 45:16-17

Do you recall the incident when James and John approached Jesus privately and asked him to promise them the places of honor, one at his right hand and the other at his left, when he came into his kingdom (MARK 10:35-40)? Jesus rebuked them for their presumption. Those places were, as we might say, assigned seats. But the sons of Zebedee were right about one thing: they would one day reign with Jesus in glory over the whole new creation. And so will we.

Here is another truth that fills us with assurance. If Christ is King, then our world is also secure. Recently I happened to read a news story entitled, "Ten Things to Scratch from Your Worry List." It was all about popular fears that aren't proven and for which there is no real evidence, like getting cancer from using your cell phone. But there are plenty of real threats out there for us to fear. Scratch ten things from your worry list and I can quickly give you ten more to replace them.

If you are worried sick, even scared to death about all the things that can go wrong in your life or in the world, let me encourage you right now to pause, take a breath, and remind yourself that Jesus is on the throne. Then ask yourself this—who really controls what happens to you? Is it blind chance? Not a chance! The universe is not governed by fate, nor do our lives play out merely according to the laws of physics and chemistry. Is it the politicians who run the world? Not likely; most of them don't seem to be able to accomplish very much. Do the generals (or perhaps the terrorists on the other side) determine what's going to happen? That would be giving them both too much credit. Maybe the world is really managed by a secret cartel of international corporations, a shadowy conspiracy of the super-rich who manipulate everything behind the scenes. No, says the Bible, it's none of these earthly powers.

The Bible's final book, Revelation, tells us who is really in control. Listen to John's testimony to the things he saw and heard on the island of Patmos, when the Lord gave him a glimpse of ultimate reality.

> Then the seventh angel blew his trumpet, and there were loud voices in heaven, saying, "The kingdom of the world has become the kingdom of our Lord, and of his Christ, and he shall reign forever and ever." And the twenty-four elders who sit on their thrones before God fell on their faces and worshiped God.
>
> —*Revelation 11:15*

And again,

> Then I heard what seemed to be the voice of a great multitude, like the roar of many waters and like the sound of mighty peals of thunder, crying out, "Hallelujah! For the Lord our God the Almighty reigns."
>
> —*Revelation 19:6*

The heavenly hallelujah chorus offers us a peek behind the scenes, providing a look at who is actually managing all the action that unfolds in the drama taking place around us on the world's stage. Behind all the activity that we see and hear about, the events that dominate our television screens and newspapers, a far greater Power looms. Nothing escapes his notice, nothing can thwart his purpose.

According to the Bible, two different kingdoms exist simultaneously in the world. One is visible and appears to be all-powerful. The "kingdom of this world" encompasses all human might and authority, every earthly regime and secular institution, whether in New York or Washington, Beijing or Moscow, Jerusalem or Tehran. But these worldly kingdoms have all been placed in subjection to the authority of the other kingdom, the kingdom of God. They "have become the kingdom of our Lord, and of his Christ." And although Jesus does not yet reign openly throughout the world, although peoples and nations continue to defy or ignore him, still he is King, and one day that will be made clear to everyone. Even now it is the Lord Jesus who actually rules, everywhere and over everyone, even if we can't see that with our physical eyes.

Christ Is Coming Again

But some day we will see it, and so will the whole creation. We will know that Jesus is king, not just by faith, but by sight. According to the New Testament, the king whose throne is eternal is going to return to earth publicly, visibly, and triumphantly to destroy all evil powers and reign openly over the universe. "Jesus shall reign where'er the Sun/Does his successive journeys run," as Isaac Watts paraphrased yet another royal psalm, Psalm 72. The end of the world means the triumphant return of the Lord Jesus Christ, and then the kingdom of this world will fully become the kingdom of our Lord, and of his Christ, and he *shall* reign forever and ever (REVELATION 11:15).

As Christians we too read the royal psalms in anticipation, just like our Jewish brothers and sisters. We too look eagerly for the final coming of the king, and the fulfillment of his promised reign of eternal peace and joy. But there is this one difference: we already know his name. We love him and serve him even now. We know that when he comes, it won't be for the first time. He came once to save, he's coming again to reign. Jesus is the once and future king.

> The King shall come when morning dawns
> And light triumphant breaks,
> When beauty gilds the eastern hills
> And life to joy awakes.
>
> Not as of old a little child,
> To bear and fight and die,
> But crowned with glory like the sun
> That lights the morning sky.

The King shall come when morning dawns
And light and beauty brings.
Hail, Christ the Lord! Your people pray:
Come quickly, King of kings.

—John Brownlie (1859–1925)

Oh, and don't forget—while we pray, "*Maranatha,* Our Lord, Come!" we also need to preach. We have to share the gospel with people everywhere. So we say to our unbelieving friends, "Dear heathen, why don't you believe the truth, renounce your idols, and take Christ into your hearts and Christianity into your temples?" And we make small personal sacrifices so that the gospel can be taken everywhere, even to the ends of the earth. This gospel we proclaim is the good news that Christ loves us, that he died and rose to save us, that he reigns now in heaven over the whole creation and that he will come again to make all things new in the consummation. On that day there won't be a foot of ground anywhere that needs a missionary.

But meanwhile, plenty of places do, so let's get going.

Study Questions

1. Explain the significance behind the comparison between Jesus and the angels in Hebrews 1. Could this comparison prove useful today in discussions with Jews and Muslims? Why or why not?

2. What does it mean to say "Christ is King"? What does it mean to you personally?

3. How, exactly, does Christ's kingship fill us with assurance? Connect the dots between the starting point of Christ being King and you living an anxiety-free life.

4. What are some of the ways that Jesus' future earthly reign will contrast with our current experience of politics as usual? How might the very institution of government be altered by Christ's kingship?

Chapter 8

Christ Our Hope

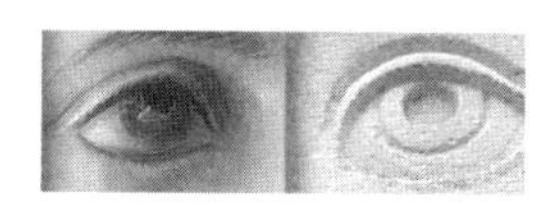

PSALM 8
HEBREWS 2:5-9

O LORD, our Lord,
how majestic is your name in all the earth! . . .

When I look at your heavens, the work of your fingers,
the moon and the stars, which you have set in place,
what is man that you are mindful of him,
and the son of man that you care for him?

Yet you have made him a little lower than the heavenly beings
and crowned him with glory and honor. . . .

O LORD, our Lord,
how majestic is your name in all the earth!

—*Psalm 8*

Now it was not to angels that God subjected the world to come, of which we are speaking. It has been testified somewhere,
"What is man, that you are mindful of him,
or the son of man, that you care for him?
You made him for a little while lower than the angels;

you have crowned him with glory and honor,
putting everything in subjection under his feet."

Now in putting everything in subjection to him, he left nothing outside his control. At present, we do not yet see everything in subjection to him. But we see him who for a little while was made lower than the angels, namely Jesus, crowned with glory and honor because of the suffering of death, so that by the grace of God he might taste death for everyone.

—Hebrews 2:5-9

ALBERTUS C. VAN RAALTE was one of the great leaders in the history of the Reformed Church in America. In 1847 he led a band of pilgrims from the Netherlands to the sandy shores of Lake Michigan in Western Michigan, where he founded the city of Holland. Van Raalte served as leader of the colony and pastor of the First Reformed Church until his death in 1876. Ten years earlier, as Van Raalte founded the institution that would eventually become Hope College, he explained his choice of the name by saying, "This is my anchor of hope for this people in the future."[21] Van Raalte's statement contains an allusion to a wonderful metaphor in the book of Hebrews for Christ.

We have this as a sure and steadfast anchor of the soul, a hope that enters into the inner place behind the curtain, where Jesus has gone as a forerunner on our behalf, having become a high priest forever after the order of Melchizedek.

—Hebrews 6:19-20

We note in passing the now-familiar quotation from Psalm 110:4. But what does the writer mean by his reference to hope as an anchor of the soul? An anchor, connected to its ship by a rope, will hold that ship in the place where it is fixed. Jesus, our anchor of hope, has gone into the inner sanctuary of heaven—the very throne room of God—and if we remain connected to him by faith, we will someday be brought to where he is. Jesus is our hope.

In Praise of Humanity

The theme of Christ our hope is developed by the writer to the Hebrews in another place as well, with reference to yet another psalm. Psalm 8 is an anthem in praise both of God and of humankind, the most exalted of all God's earthly creatures. That's according to the Bible; this view of a special high status for human beings is increasingly rejected by atheists and materialists today. But even as believers we often find it difficult to imagine we occupy a unique place in the universe. Who hasn't sat outside on some brilliant, starlit night and repeated the psalmist's wondering question: "When I consider the heavens, the moon and the stars, what is man?" We are dwarfed by the immensity of a seemingly infinite universe that appears to be indifferent to our presence in it. Compared to the vastness of time and space, we seem to ourselves like specks of dust, with the lifespan of a mayfly. How could even the greatest and most famous of humans possibly matter in a 14-billion-year-old universe that's home to 10-thousand-million galaxies?

But the psalmist says we matter very much. In fact, he says we are crowned with glory and honor. Only a little lower in rank than the angels of heaven, we humans have been placed by God over the whole earth and all its creatures. In language that echoes God's creation commands to our first parents to fill the earth and rule over it, the psalmist praises God for the authority he has given to humankind:

> You have given him dominion over the works of your hands;
>   you have put all things under his feet,
> all sheep and oxen,
>   and also the beasts of the field,
> the birds of the heavens, and the fish of the sea,
>   whatever passes along the paths of the seas.
>
> —*Psalm 8:6-8*

That's an astonishing statement. God has entrusted his whole creation, says the psalmist—"the works of [his] hands . . . all things"—to us! What an honor, and what a responsibility. God sees human beings as important enough to rule over the entire universe, and as responsible enough to take good care of that tiny corner of it in which he has placed us for now.

The Problem of Psalm 8

Psalm 8 affirms these truths about the dignity and importance of human beings without qualification. That's why it uses the old-fashioned generic term "man" to make the point. It's not just this special person or that one who is crowned with glory and ennobled with status and authority. It is *man* who is thus honored; human beings in general, each and every one of us. Even the lowliest among us is a god-like creature, worthy of great honor. This raises a problem, because it doesn't seem like this psalm is telling the truth. We—all of us—are great and glorious creatures, whose destiny is to rule the universe? You must be kidding! Just look at reality.

We live in a world where human beings are regularly trampled upon, systematically used up and discarded, and then thrown away like yesterday's trash. In fact, the large majority of the world's people spend their lives in anonymous squalor and suffering. How exalted is it to be a person who lives his life in a shanty on a garbage dump in Manila or Mexico City? How honored is a life as an enslaved child prostitute in Bangkok?

Moreover, for those of us who are powerful and wealthy in global terms (which pretty much includes anyone reading these words) our so-called "rule" over the earth often takes the form of exploitation and abuse. We suck oil from the ground like a cloud of hungry mosquitoes swarming on unprotected skin. We pollute air and water in our quest for even more wealth, most of which we spend in the self-centered pursuit of pleasure. Our supposed "care" of God's creation, our rule over our fellow creatures, has resulted in mass exterminations and potentially irreparable harm to our beautiful planet.

Furthermore, where is the harmony of nature? If God has placed all things in subjection under us, including the beasts of the field and the fish of the sea, then why do lions and tigers and sharks try to eat us? For that matter, why do dogs snarl and bark at us? Why do hurricanes and tornadoes batter us, and earthquakes shake us, and tsunamis pound us, and eruptions bury us? Why do cancers ravage us, and strokes cripple us, and heart attacks fell us, and age enfeeble us?

Most problematic of all, what about death? Where did that come from? We live in a world where, from the first moment we draw breath, death is stalking us. How can we believe in our own importance and dignity when at every turn we're confronted with that hideous reality? Death mocks all our pretensions. It snuffs out our hopes and dreams. It puts an end to everything we love. It shows us how small and insignificant and powerless we are, how meaningless our lives turn out to be in the end. Death is the great enemy, not just to physical life, but to the very possibility that we have any lasting purpose or significance at all.

Obviously, something has gone wrong. The psalmist isn't lying to us. We do have this exalted place in God's plan of creation. But things are out of kilter in the world, at least temporarily. Something has entered our world that has disrupted its natural order and distorted God's original intention for his creation. If you know the whole story of the Bible, then you know that this distorting, disrupting "something" is human sin, sin that has given birth to the great destroyer, death. And if you know the whole story of the Bible, then you also know that God has addressed this problem. In fact, he's done something to solve it.

Christ in this Psalm

We have been looking at how various New Testament writers quote from the Psalms to show that they speak directly of the Lord Jesus Christ. Psalm 8 is also quoted directly in the New Testament, but the way Christ is seen here is highly significant. In the second chapter of the letter to the Hebrews the writer introduces an idea that brings to light the deeper meaning of Psalm 8. He begins with a rather vague introduction. "Someone somewhere has written," he says—a phrase that comforts anyone who has ever tried to recall an exact Bible reference! "It has been testified somewhere," he writes,

> 'What is man, that you are mindful of him,
> or the son of man, that you care for him?
> You made him for a little while lower than the angels;
> you have crowned him with glory and honor,
> putting everything in subjection under his feet.'
>
> Now in putting everything in subjection to him, he left nothing outside his control. At present, we do not yet see everything in subjection to him. But we see him who for a little while was made lower than the angels, namely Jesus, crowned with glory and honor because of the suffering of death, so that by the grace of God he might taste death for everyone.
>
> —*Hebrews 2:6-9*

If you have been paying attention so far, you recognized that Hebrews is quoting Psalm 8. And if you read the above passage closely, you noticed that the writer quotes the psalm with a slight variation: "you made him *for a little while* lower than the angels . . ." In Hebrews' reading of this text the psalmist is not talking simply about men in general, but about one man in particular. The "son of man" that God cares for is actually *the* Son of Man, Jesus Christ; the representative human being, the "Proper Man," as Luther called him. It is Jesus who fulfills our human destiny for us and guarantees that we will eventually realize it ourselves. He occupies the rightful place for all humanity that God intended from the beginning. He is the second Adam, who succeeds where the first one failed. He takes on human nature, becoming for a little while lower than the angels. He obeys perfectly. All things are subject to him, even in his humanity. ("What sort of man is this," they asked, "that even the wind and the waves obey him?") He suffers and he dies. But then he is raised and crowned with glory and honor. And he has done it all for us, to enable us to share his righteousness, and some day his glory and authority too.

THINGS AT PRESENT

We cannot see this truth, though, in our death-dominated world. In what must rank as one of the all-time understatements, Hebrews 2:8 states, "At present, we do not yet see everything in subjection to him" (either to "man" or to *the* Man, Christ Jesus). What a world of frustration and pain, of sin and rebellion, suffering and tragedy, is hinted at in that matter-of-fact sentence! But don't judge things prematurely. They will turn out different than they presently appear.

So we don't see all things in subjection at the moment, but, Hebrews hastens to add, we do see this: "We see him who for a little while was made lower than the angels, namely Jesus, crowned with glory and honor because of the suffering of death, so that by the grace of God he might taste death for everyone" (V. 9). As it is, we do not yet see everything in subjection to him—or to us. Evil and suffering remain, and death seems to hold sway in our world. The Lord's rule is not yet acknowledged by all; and his will continues to be resisted, especially by "the rulers . . . the authorities . . . the cosmic powers over this present darkness . . . the spiritual forces of evil in the heavenly places" (EPHESIANS 6:12). But we do see this: we see Jesus, who died for us to set us free from sin and death, now raised and exalted in glory. It's the Resurrection that is our guarantee, both of Christ's final authority and of our final victory.

DOMINI SUMUS

In 1534 Martin Luther wrote a comforting letter to his brother-in-law, a fellow scholar, who was seriously ill. Luther sought to encourage the sick man by reminding him that we are always in the Lord's hands. "We are his at all times," he wrote, "as Saint Paul says, 'whether we live or die, we are the Lord's.'" But then Luther goes on to make a further point from this text—Romans 14:8—which he had quoted in Latin. The Latin word for "Lord's" in that verse, *Domini,* could be translated two ways; either as a possessive ("Lord's" with an apostrophe) or as a simple plural ("lords" without the apostrophe). "Yes, indeed," exclaimed Luther,

> "We are the Lord's" because we are his dwelling place, his members, and . . . "we are lords" because we rule over all things through faith, which is our victory, and because, thanks be to God, we trample the lion and the dragon underfoot. In short, says Jesus, "Be of good cheer; I have overcome the world."[22]

This is the fantastic message of Christ our hope: *Domini Sumus.* We are *the Lord's* and we are *the lords,* both in the possessive and in the plural. Because we are the Lord's, we are also the lords over the whole creation. Because Christ has defeated evil, we will one day see all things in subjection to him, and to us. Because Christ tasted death for us, we will be raised to reign with him. And all our hopes and dreams will be more than realized. The proof that all this will come to pass is Jesus himself, once humbled but now exalted, whom we see at present with the eyes of faith, reigning in glory.

The Reverend Abraham Polhemus was at the height of his career when he accepted the call to become the pastor of the North Reformed Church in Newark, a prominent and flourishing congregation in New Jersey's biggest city. Shortly after Polhemus arrived, the church began to build a large and impressive new building in the heart of the city, which still stands there 150 years later. But their new pastor did not live to see it completed. Stricken with a fatal illness, Abraham Polhemus died in 1857 at the age of 45. To the left of the pulpit, on the sanctuary wall, hangs a marble plaque erected by the congregation in Polhemus's memory. "He laid the foundations of this edifice," it reads,

> but his voice was never heard within its walls. When the time of his departure was at hand, in faith he exclaimed: "that church shall be erected, souls there shall be converted to Christ, and I shall rejoice over them in Heaven." Of a noble nature, embellished by culture and grace—frank and disinterested as a man—sagacious and prudent as a counselor—eloquent and scriptural, exemplary and devoted as a minister of Christ, he was very dear to his people, and beloved by the Church at large. His brief ministry here will not be forgotten. His memory is a

> rich legacy. Called hence in the vigor of manhood, surrounded by all the attractions of life, he received the message with joy, and as heaven was opening to his view, exclaimed: "I see Jesus, and my soul is ravished by the sight."

Whatever our circumstances or condition, with Hebrews, and with Abraham Polhemus, and with the saints through the ages, we can say, "At present, we do not yet see everything in subjection to him. *But we see . . . Jesus.*" And *he* is our ultimate anchor of hope for the future.

Study Questions

1. How has Jesus been your anchor of hope? What are you tempted to substitute as your anchor from time to time?

2. Psalm 8 captures well both the insignificance and the grandeur we can experience at times. But it also affirms that we have been given significant tasks to perform in our capacity as rulers with God. Does this mean that all forms of work are equal in God's eyes? Is God indifferent about whether people are doctors, lawyers, preachers, or plumbers?

3. As rulers over God's world, we are called to be wise and effective stewards of all that God has created. How does that stewardship responsibility extend to our neighbor, the environment, the poor, and to institutions such as the church and the family?

4. What's unique about the way Christ is presented in Hebrews 2, especially given the backdrop of Psalm 8?

5. Explain in your own words the significance of Martin Luther's point about the Latin phrase *Domini Sumus* (from Romans 14:8): "We are *the Lord's* and we are *the lords.*"

Chapter 9

CHRIST THE CORNERSTONE

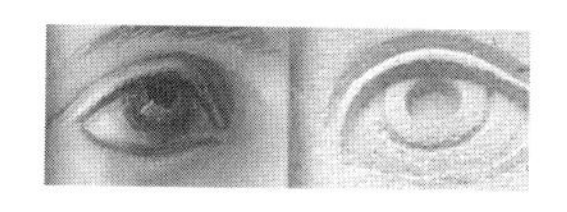

PSALM 118:22-23
MARK 12:1-12
1 PETER 2:4-7

The stone that the builders rejected
    has become the cornerstone.
This is the LORD's doing;
    it is marvelous in our eyes.

—Psalm 118:22-23

As you come to him, a living stone rejected by men but in the sight of God chosen and precious, you yourselves like living stones are being built up as a spiritual house, to be a holy priesthood, to offer spiritual sacrifices acceptable to God through Jesus Christ. For it stands in Scripture:

"Behold, I am laying in Zion a stone,
    a cornerstone chosen and precious,
and whoever believes in him will not be put to shame."

So the honor is for you who believe, but for those who do not believe,

> "The stone that the builders rejected
> has become the cornerstone,"

—1 Peter 2:4-7

On a Saturday night in December, 2007, a young man named Matthew Murray entered a YWAM (Youth With a Mission) training center near Boulder, Colorado. Murray, who had previously spent four months as a trainee in the center, shot and killed two staff members there. Sometime later that night he drove to the campus of New Life Church, a megachurch in Colorado Springs, where on Sunday morning he killed two teenage sisters in the parking lot. Entering the church's lobby, Murray was confronted and fired upon by a security guard, whereupon he turned his gun on himself and took his own life. A letter was found in his car, addressed to God. "Why didn't any changes occur or any love or help come when I accepted you as Lord and Savior?" wrote Murray.[23]

Christians can sometimes be guilty of false advertising. We can so emphasize the victory of Christ, paint so glowing a picture of the new life, talk so confidently about the power of the Spirit, that we shatter the faith and destroy the hope of people who don't feel very powerful or experience much victory. Yes, it is possible to so stress the truth of justification that we downplay the need for sanctification and leave people complacent in their sins. But it is also possible to lead people to believe that if they pray regularly and follow a few simple rules they will have total deliverance. We must be honest both in teaching biblical truth and in sharing our own spiritual struggles. The Christian life is not a snap. Personal change and growth in holiness do not come quickly or easily. When I survey my own inward heart, I am tempted to think that none of the glowing promises of victory are true, or at least that they are not meant for me. But when I feel discouraged because of the stubbornness of my own sins, I need to acknowledge that I do love God, and I do trust in Christ. John Bunyan shares this kind of honest testimony in the conclusion to his spiritual autobiography, *Grace Abounding to the Chief of Sinners.*

> I have wondered much at this one thing, that though God doth visit my soul with never so blessed a discovery of himself, yet I have found again that such hours have attended me afterwards, that I have been in my spirit so filled with darkness, that I could not so much as once conceive what that God and that comfort was with which I have been refreshed. I have sometimes seen more in a line of the Bible than I could well tell how to stand under and yet at another time the whole Bible hath been to me as dry as a stick . . . . Of all tears they are the best that are made by the blood of Christ; and of all joy, that is the sweetest that is mixed with mourning over Christ: O, 'tis a goodly thing to be on our knees with Christ in our arms before God. I hope I know something of these things.[24]

I love that last line especially: "I hope I know something of these things." That's a modest testimony. It is the antithesis of spiritual triumphalism. We must take great care not to make Christ a stumbling block to struggling people, or create a false impression about the true nature of the Christian life. The walk of faith is an up and down journey, feelings of love for God come and go, battles against sin are lost as often as they are won. The one constant is Jesus, the God who is for us and with us. I can't point to very much in my life or character that gives incontrovertible evidence to the power of Christ to save and the love of Christ to transform. But I too hope I know something of these things. I still confess that he is my Cornerstone. I will stake my future on his promises, and I will live and die trying to follow him. And every time I approach the throne of God, it is on my knees with Christ in my arms.

Happy Endings?

Everybody loves a story with a happy ending. Talk of a stone that is rejected by the builders but turns into the cornerstone of the entire edifice sounds like this kind of story. Such tales are familiar to us: the ugly duckling—gawky, gangly, *different*—that grows up to be a beautiful swan; Rudolph, who stands out because of his big red nose, who is never allowed to join in any reindeer games—until that fateful foggy Christmas Eve, "when Santa came to say. . . ." These are stories where former rejects are welcomed, accepted, valued; of course we love them.

But let's be honest. The kind of happy endings childrens' stories feature rarely play out that way in real life. In our experience, ugly ducklings don't usually turn into swans. They grow up to be lonely adults. Misfits don't happen to discover a unique skill that makes them popular overnight. They struggle with rage and hatred, directed against others but often themselves as well. And sometimes they pick up a gun and start shooting in a church parking lot, or on a school campus.

"The stone that the builders rejected" that "has become the cornerstone" is not a biblical version of the story of the ugly duckling. It isn't a story of a happy ending, at least not in the fairy tale sense. The stone is Jesus. The rejection is how most responded to him, expressed finally by his crucifixion. The message of the text is not "everybody changed their opinion about him when they saw what he was really like." The message is about the stark contrast between the way the majority of Jesus' contemporaries evaluated him and the way God did. "You crucified him," as Peter would declare, "but God raised him up" (see ACTS 2:23-24). Unbelief rejected—and still rejects—Jesus, but God has vindicated him, and made him the foundation and cornerstone of the church (see 1 CORINTHIANS 3:11, EPHESIANS 2:20). "This is the LORD'S doing; it is marvelous in our eyes" (PSALM 118:23).

Jesus' Final Days

Psalm 118:22 figures prominently in one story from the Passion Week narrative in the Gospels. According to the Gospel record, two things brought the hatred and fear of Jesus' enemies to a boiling point and made them finally decide it was time to get rid of Jesus for good. The first was Jesus' final miracle when he raised his friend Lazarus from the dead. The news of this astonishing act swept through the city of Jerusalem and its environs like a desert brush fire, causing a near panic among the members of the Jewish ruling council. "What are we to do," they asked themselves, "For this man performs many signs. If we let him go on like this, everyone will believe in him, and the Romans will come and take away both our place and our nation" (JOHN 11:47-48).

The solution was proposed by Caiaphas, the chief priest, who observed that it was better for one man to die than for everyone to be jeopardized—typical political expediency, in other words. "So from that day on," the Gospel of John says, "they made plans to put him to death" (V. 53). Jesus' judicial murder was motivated in the first place by the fear his popularity triggered in the elite members of society—fear that he would upset the social order and cost them their privileged positions, which is just about the commonest motive there is for getting rid of anyone who challenges the system.

But something else happened that made the rulers in Jerusalem determine to kill Jesus without further delay, something, in fact, that turned their cold calculation into white-hot anger. It was simply a story that Jesus told shortly after raising Lazarus from the dead. The first three Gospels all tell how Jesus rode into the holy city triumphantly on Palm Sunday, and then the next day cleared out all the money changers and peddlers who had turned the temple into what he called "a den of robbers." The chief priests, elders, and teachers of the law—in other words, the entire power structure of the city—all were offended by this act. Those three groups included everybody who mattered in Jerusalem society. They represented both Sadducees and Pharisees, two normally antagonistic parties who had joined in an informal alliance to deal with the threat that Jesus posed.

So when Jesus and his disciples entered Jerusalem again on Tuesday of Holy Week and went once more into the temple courts, the leaders of the Sadducees and Pharisees were waiting for him. They confronted Jesus: "By what authority are you doing these things?" they demanded (MARK 11:28). In other words, what right did Jesus have to walk around the temple like he owned the place?

But of course, that is exactly what he did—he owned the place! After all, it was his Father's house.

A History of Israel

To answer his enemies' challenge Jesus tells them a parable with a very sharp point (MARK 12:1-12). It was all about the owner of a vineyard who rented it out to a group of tenant farmers. The owner went away to live in another country, and sent his servants periodically to collect the rent that was due to him. But the tenants abused and rejected those servants, refusing their demands, until finally the owner tried sending his own son to the vineyard in hopes that he would receive more respect. But the tenants killed him and threw him out of the vineyard.

Now comes the point of the story. Jesus asks a rhetorical question, "What will the owner of the vineyard do?" And he answers, "He will come and destroy the tenants and give the vineyard to others" (V. 9). And then Jesus quotes Psalm 118 to these members of the establishment, men who are in the process of acting out in real life the story that he's just told them in parable form. "Have you not read this Scripture:" [Jesus asks]

> "The stone that the builders rejected
> has become the cornerstone." (PSALM 118:22)

When Jesus finished speaking his audience knew exactly what he was getting at. They understood his story perfectly. "They were seeking to arrest him," the Gospel writer says, "for they perceived that he had told the parable against them" (V. 12).

But do we understand as clearly what Jesus meant? Are we as quick as his enemies to get his point? While Jesus' parables were sometimes obscure to his audience, in this case his meaning was transparent and instantly grasped. Everybody recognized it because the story he told was based on a familiar Old Testament passage, in Isaiah 5, which describes Israel as God's vineyard. So the people understood who was who. The vineyard was Israel; the tenants were the leaders, especially those priests and scribes and Pharisees; the servants sent by the owner were the Old Testament prophets who spoke God's word to the people. And, of course, the son who came in the end to the vineyard was Jesus himself.

The story Jesus tells is really the story of the Bible; it is a metaphorical history of Israel. As such, it is a history of persistent mercy met by persistent rejection. God sent messenger after messenger to his people, all of them asking for the return that was due to him by right, namely, the fruit of repentance, of love, of gratitude and the obedience of personal and social justice. But the message was spurned and the messengers shamefully treated. How could the Lord continue to send prophet after prophet, and in the end his only Son? Doesn't he know what's going to happen? Yet still God's messengers call out with his word of grace and his invitation to respond. "Mercy," said the great 19th-century evangelical bishop J. C. Ryle, "is God's darling attribute."

But mercy, broad and deep as it is, is not forever. Persistent rejection eventually meets with hard judgment. That too is the message of Jesus. It's not all grace, all the time. Eventually the time to respond runs out and the day of salvation draws to a close, and those who have rejected the Son meet with a terrible doom. If the people reject their Messiah, Jesus warns, God will destroy their nation and give his kingdom to others. The people of God would henceforth be the church, the body of those, both Jews and Gentiles, who believe in Christ Jesus. For Israel's chief priests and rulers and teachers of the law the day of reckoning was close at hand.

Stumbling Block or Capstone?

Jesus' listeners were so enthralled by the story he told that day in the temple courtyard that they put themselves right into the middle of it. They had ceased to be merely an audience; they had themselves been caught up as actors in the story. And something like that needs to happen to each of us as well. We must read this parable not just as a metaphor about first-century Israel, but as a confrontation with our own destiny. Put simply, the message is this: your eternal fate will be determined by your attitude toward Jesus Christ. That point is driven home by that brief verse from Psalm 118. "The stone the builders rejected has become the cornerstone [or 'the capstone']" (V. 22).

The capstone of an arch is the central stone at the top that holds all the others together; remove that one stone and the whole structure collapses. The cornerstone of the building is the key to the whole foundation; the entire structure is based upon it. But a rejected stone becomes a stumbling block, a stone that causes you to trip and fall—or that falls on you. Jesus closed his parable of the tenants in the vineyard with these words of warning: "And the one who falls on this stone will be broken to pieces; and when it falls on anyone, it will crush him" (MATTHEW 21:44).

No Other Name

So the very same stone is either the crucial element in one's life or the cause of untold, infinite disaster, and it all depends on whether that stone is accepted or rejected. Jesus Christ is both. He is the cornerstone or he is the stumbling block. Psalm 118 is talking about him and the decisive role he plays in every single person's life. The New Testament makes this fact perfectly clear.

The story is told of an occasion when Thomas Aquinas, the greatest theologian of the Middle Ages, was visiting Rome. The pope himself received Thomas and undertook to show him some of the treasures of the Vatican. "As you see," said the pontiff with evident satisfaction, "the Church can no longer say, 'Silver and gold have I none.'" "No," Thomas immediately replied, "and neither can she say, 'In the name of the Lord Jesus, rise up and walk!'"

The pope and the theologian were both alluding to an incident from the earliest history of the church, which is described in Acts 3. As Peter and John were entering the temple in Jerusalem one afternoon, a crippled beggar who was sitting by the gate asked them for alms. Peter looked at him and said, "I have no silver and gold, but what I do have I give to you. In the name of Jesus Christ of Nazareth, rise up and walk!" (ACTS 3:6). The man not only got right up and started to walk; he "entered the temple with them, walking and leaping and praising God" (V. 8). Peter took advantage of the crowd that gathered to witness this amazing sight—the crippled beggar was a well-known figure to all the temple's regular visitors—to do what he was always doing in those days. He preached the gospel to them. So the temple guard arrested the disciples, and the next day they were hauled before the Jewish Council.

This council, remember, was the very same body that had condemned Jesus to death a short time before. But Peter was undaunted. You want to know about the healing?, he asked. It happened by the name of Jesus Christ of Nazareth, the same Jesus you crucified and God raised from the dead. "This Jesus is the stone that was rejected by you, the builders, which has become the cornerstone. And there is no other name under heaven given among men by which we must be saved" (ACTS 4:11-12). Years later Peter amplified that message in his first epistle.

> As you come to him, a living stone rejected by men but in the sight of God chosen and precious, you yourselves like living stones are being built up as a spiritual house, to be a holy priesthood, to offer spiritual sacrifices acceptable to God through Jesus Christ. For it stands in Scripture:
>
> "Behold, I am laying in Zion a stone,
> a cornerstone chosen and precious,
> and whoever believes in him will not be put to shame."
>
> So the honor is for you who believe. But for those who do not believe,
>
> "The stone that the builders rejected
> has become the cornerstone" —*1 Peter 2:4-7*

Either/Or

It all comes down to what has been called the "scandal of particularity." Is salvation really through Christ alone? Must everyone accept the Lord Jesus to be saved? Why should that be? Why just him, why only one way? Why can't you find God in your way, and I in mine? Why this insistence on the cross, and the blood, and acceptance of Christian doctrine, and personal trust in Christ and all the rest? I sometimes wonder, though, whether these commonly raised objections are really just a smokescreen. Because the crucial question isn't really whether everyone accepts Christ. The crucial question is whether *you* do.

Many people today who express interest in religion (or, as they are more likely to say, in spirituality) want something that's hip and eclectic and ethically appealing—humanitarianism with occasional references to Jesus, Buddha, or Mohammed mixed in. The great majority of Americans believe in God, in the sense that they acknowledge the existence of an easy-going, all-accepting "Higher Power." But biblical Christianity offers a crucified Christ and a hard choice: make him the cornerstone of your life, or he will become a stumbling block that will break you. Build your life on Christ, or his judgment will crush you. That's not a scare tactic; it's just plain reality. Jesus Christ is either the salvation or destruction of every last human life.

We don't say this with any sense of relish. No Christian can delight in the thought of anyone being lost forever. Nor do we presume to judge any individual's destiny; only God knows enough to do that. But we do stress the biblical either/or with respect to Jesus Christ: either stake your all upon him—no matter what, to the very end—or face eternal ruin. This we must say to one and all.

Mostly, though, we say it to ourselves as followers of Christ. People are rarely frightened into the kingdom by the prospect of judgment, but many would-be followers do drop out when they discover that the gate is narrow and the way is hard, and the payoff isn't always obvious or the rewards immediate. As G. K. Chesterton pungently remarked, "Christianity hasn't been tried and found wanting; it's been found hard and hasn't been tried." The primary reason for accepting Jesus as *your* Lord and Savior is just that he is *the* Lord and Savior—not so that he can solve your personal problems or give you a successful life. Believe the gospel because it is true, not because it's helpful, at least helpful in ways you can immediately see and appreciate.

At the end of the 6th century, just before the rise of Islam would forever sweep away the Christian Byzantine Empire in the Middle East, a Greek monk named John Moschos traveled on foot from Greece to Egypt, passing through Turkey, Syria and Palestine en route. He stayed in monasteries along the way, visiting hermits in their caves and speaking with abbots and holy brothers, collecting their stories and sayings. Moschos wrote these down in a book that he called *The Spiritual Meadow.* This is story #208.

> A brother who was in the grips of depression asked an elder; "What am I to do; for I am assailed by doubts which say to me, 'You became a monk in vain: you shall not be saved'?" The elder replied, "You know, brother, even if we cannot enter the promised land, it is better for our bones to fall in the wilderness than for us to turn back to Egypt."[25]

As I read that I think of C. S. Lewis's remark that if the gospel isn't true, it ought to be, because it's a better story than any reality the world has to offer. What Lewis is saying is that the gospel isn't too good to be true; it's so good it *has* to be true. I also think of Peter's haunting question to Jesus, "Lord, to whom shall we go? You have the words of eternal life" (JOHN 6:68). If you want to have any hope at all, there is no alternative to Jesus Christ.

So let's do this right now. Let's resolve to trust fully in Christ and believe all that the psalms and the rest of the Bible say about him. Let's commit ourselves to following him all our days, with no turning back. And let's go on in the confidence that, in Bunyan's words from *Grace Abounding,* "the Milk and Honey is beyond this Wilderness."

Study Questions

1. Have you ever experienced Christian teaching that so stressed the truth of justification that it downplayed the need for ongoing sanctification? What effect did this have on your relationship with Christ?

2. Recount the irony in Jesus' quotation of Psalm 118:22 to the religious leaders in Mark 12:1-12. Why were they so upset with Jesus? See also Isaiah 5.

3. Why is it true to say, following the great 19th-century evangelical Bishop J. C. Ryle, "Mercy is God's darling attribute"?

4. Explain how Jesus Christ can be either the cornerstone or the stumbling block of your life. Provide appropriate illustrations if possible.

5. How do you respond when you hit a stretch of spiritual wilderness? Do you admit it? Do you try to act like it doesn't exist? Do you ask God to deliver you from it, and then believe that he will in time?

ENDNOTES

1. John Donne, *Sermons on the Psalms and Gospels,* ed. Evelyn Simpson, Berkeley: University of California, 1963, p. 94.

2. St. Athanasius, "Letter to Marcellinus," appendix to *On the Incarnation,* St. Vladimir's Seminary Press, Crestwood, NY, 1993, pp. 103, 105.

3. St. Athanasius, *ibid.,* p. 99ff.

4. Artur Weiser, *The Psalms,* Philadelphia: Westminster, 1962, p. 112.

5. Weiser, *ibid,* p. 112.

6. Flannery O'Connor, *Collected Works,* New York: Library of America, 1988, p. 152.

7. J. I. Packer, "The Heart of the Gospel," *In My Place Condemned He Stood,* Wheaton: Crossway, 2008, p. 32; (reprinted from *Knowing God*, Downers Grove: InterVarsity Press, 1993.)

8. Packer, *ibid,* p. 22.

9. Packer, *ibid,* p. 21.

10. Michael Wilcock, *The Message of Psalms 1-72,* Downers Grove: InterVarsity Press, 2001, p. 147.

11. *Eusebius—The Church History: A New Translation with Commentary,* translated and edited by Paul L. Maier, Grand Rapids: Kregel, 1999, p. 269.

12. John Stott, *The Cross of Christ,* Downers Grove, InterVarsity Press, 1986, p. 81.

13. "Sermon Preached to the Earl of Carlisle," *John Donne: The Major Works,* John Carey, ed., Oxford: Oxford University Press, 2000, p. 318ff.

14. Peter Taylor Forsyth, *The Justification of God,* Blackwood, Australia: New Creation Publications, 1988, p. 223 (reprinted edition, originally published in 1917).

15. From David Heller's collection of children's letters to God, *Dear God: What Religion Were the Dinosaurs?;* quoted in *Christian Home and School,* January/February 1991, p. 21.

16. St. Athanasius, op. cit., p. 50.

17. John Bunyan, *The Pilgrim's Progress,* (Second Part), Penguin Books Ltd., 1965, p. 225.

18. N. T. Wright, Closing Address to Anglican Consultative Council, 6/28/05, accessed online: http://www.ntwrightpage.com/Wright_Shipwreck_Kingdom.htm.

19. C. S. Lewis, "The Psalms," *Christian Reflections,* Grand Rapids: Eerdmans, 1994, p. 114.

20. Originally quoted in *Princeton Seminary: Faith and Learning 1812–1868,* v. 1, p. 193; accessed online at www.christkirk.com/MissionsAndChurchPlants/hodgeletter.asp.

21. www.hope.edu

22. Martin Luther, *Letters of Spiritual Counsel,* Theodore G. Tappert, ed. and trans., Vancouver, B.C.: Regent College Publishing, 2003, p. 38.

23. Quoted in *Christianity Today,* May, 2008.

24. *Selections from the Writings of John Bunyan,* Monica Furlong, ed., London: The Folio Society, 1978, p. 98.

25. John Moschos, *The Spiritual Meadow*, St. Vladimir, Crestwood, New York, 1994, p. 187.